The African Violet

THE AFRICAN

SAINTPAULIA

VIOLET

By
Helen Van Pelt Wilson

Drawings by
Léonie Hagerty

M. BARROWS
AND COMPANY, INC.
PUBLISHERS   NEW YORK

To

ELSIE CROASDALE FREED

Whose Handsome Plants and Pioneer Research
Have Extended the Saintpaulia Horizon
For Us All

Foreword

A CORDIAL welcome awaits this first book on the African violet. It will be read with delight and profit too, by all who love the saintpaulia and have wanted to know more about this beautiful house plant which in recent years has received so much attention—scientifically, aesthetically, and commercially.

As a writer on horticultural subjects, few can surpass Helen Van Pelt Wilson. Those who know her study of *Geraniums—Pelargoniums* will find here the same enlightenment on African violets, and the same enthusiastic presentation of her magazine articles and of her little pamphlet, *African Violets as a Hobby*, written in 1943. The sixty-seven detailed descriptions and the comprehensive listing of over one hundred and seventy-five varieties are particularly valuable.

The members of the African Violet Society of America, Inc. wish to express their appreciation to Helen Van Pelt Wilson for the research she has done. We will be turning often to this book to check our own findings or to compare opinions on controversial points. Just as the

African violet has become the most popular house plant in our homes, offices, and schoolrooms, this book will soon be the most popular on our garden book shelves.

FERNE KELLAR, *President*
African Violet Society of America, Inc.

September, 1947,
Des Moines, Iowa.

With Gratitude

As I MOMENTARILY close the gate today on my exploration of the saintpaulia, I feel an overwhelming sense of gratitude to the hundreds of men and women who have so generously shared their knowledge and in many ways assisted my research. Since this is the first book to be written on African violets, it would have been very limited in scope if enthusiasts in Canada, in Maine, Georgia, Iowa, Mississippi, Ohio, California, and Pennsylvania, to mention but a few places, had not come forward with accounts of their own discoveries and experiences. Three women in particular have contributed to this work.

One day when I was ill in bed, frustrated in my work by a bad cold, I answered the telephone to a pleasant voice saying, 'May I talk with you about African violets?' I soon came to know that voice well and its owner, too, for it was Elsie Freed who had called me. We were strangers then but soon akin, as plant-lovers always are, particularly if the favorite happens to be African violets, undoubtedly the ace friendship-maker among house plants.

Soon I visited Mrs. Freed and saw a collection of

saintpaulias which was astounding in its extent and quality. In her windows of every exposure African violets were growing at their most handsome best. On that April day the flowers were open in profusion and the plants beautiful in their elegance and symmetry. Mrs. Freed herself is a "natural" horticulturist with the scientist's attitude toward facts and the gardener's love of beauty. She not only permitted me to study often in her African violet "laboratory" but allowed the artist to make almost all the illustrative drawings right from her plants.

Léonie Hagerty, who, in the course of our book, became Mrs. Louis Bell, was the lady with the clever pen. When she sits down to draw a saintpaulia she does more than see it—she understands it—for she has that rare combination, artistic competence and horticultural knowledge. She is a graduate of the School of Horticulture for Women at Ambler, Pennsylvania. Léonie not only drew, she assisted with plant description, and when we developed the color chart, it was her color-conscious eye which arranged the blossoms on the table in careful and actual sequence of shade. Her cooperation and her devotion to her work—on her wedding day she sent her best-man brother with the last of the drawings—have made me unbelievably grateful.

And then there is my dear friend, Alice Bond Newnham, who has been more than secretary, really a coordinator of all the efforts necessary to the assembling of this information. Mrs. Newnham is the busy mother of two boys, but she always found time to go with me on explorations and studies of collections, to take notes, write letters—a thousand of them perhaps—and then to produce a digest of information suitable for the chapter in process. Aside from real competence, perhaps her greatest contribution was her delightful companionship in my labors, somehow making it all just fun.

To many others I send a special thank-you too, especially for help in sorting out and describing varieties. I can only mention specifically Anne Tinari (whose new greenhouse was always open to me), Mrs. Arthur Radtke, Alma Wright, R. A. Brown, R. G. Baxter, Ruth Yoars, Clarissa Harris, Jean Crowe, Ferne Kellar, Mrs. W. H. Odom, Helen Roberts Bohannon, Fay Wilcox, Pansy Barnes, Mary C. Orrell, Mrs. W. H. Cowan, Mrs. Frederic L. Beers, Jane Coleman, and Armacost and Royston.

Much general information on saintpaulias has come to me from Dr. Liberty Hyde Bailey, W. D. Holley, Charles J. Hudson, Jr., Claude Gortatowsky, Mrs. O. H. Myers, Regina Zacharias, George McFarland, the Ohio State University, the New Jersey Agricultural Experiment Station, the Missouri Botanical Gardens, and the University of Illinois.

For knowledge of greenhouse practice I want particularly to thank Faust Greenhouses, Clackamas Greenhouses, Inc., H. R. Brown, Carl J. Ulery, and especially E. C. Hunkel, who read and reread the greenhouse chapter.

I am also grateful to Marion P. Thomas, Director of Round Robins for the *Flower Grower*. She told me the story of the development of the Robins in that magazine.

I am indebted to *Better Homes and Gardens, Farm Journal,* and the *Ladies' Home Journal* for the use of material originally prepared for them.

The gate which closes on my studies today will often be opened for the quest has only just begun and I am sure the future will frequently find me strolling again down these saintpaulia paths.

HELEN VAN PELT WILSON

August, 1947,
Germantown, Philadelphia.

Contents

Illustrations

The African Violet

CHAPTER ONE

Early Days

To EVERY lover of "green things growing" the African violet offers a challenge. It will grow well and bloom almost endlessly under the conditions of the average dwelling, but it will not flourish so easily as to let us neglect it or lose interest in it. At its best the saintpaulia is a great delight and particularly dear to all of us who need flowering plants at the window to call a house a home.

Some fifty years ago this "violet" was discovered in "the hilly regions of Eastern tropical Africa." Today it is the darling of the window-garden enthusiast and the profitable joy of the florist as well. On greenhouse benches and the housewife's sill, it blooms with equal grace, increasing its original popularity of 1893 when, for the first time, it flowered in Europe, thousands of miles from its native haunts.

From the day of its discovery, the saintpaulia took the horticultural world by storm. An important garden magazine of the time noted, beside the drawing we have reproduced: "It does not often happen that a plant newly introduced into Europe can claim the honor accorded to the subject of this plate, of being within two

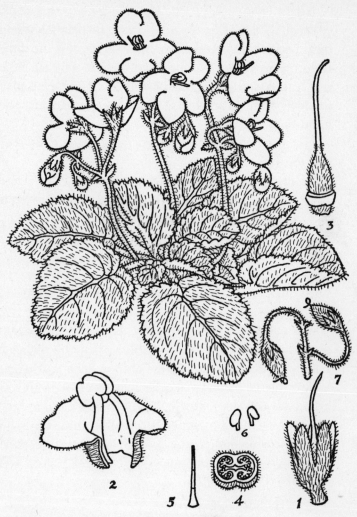

Saintpaulia ionantha. 1. calyx and style; 2. tube
of corolla laid open and stamen; 3. ovary and
disk; 4. transverse section of ovary; 5. hair of
margin of corolla; 6. ovules; 7. immature fruit.

years of its flowering figured in five first-class horticultural periodicals." And today in America, it is the same.
Leading magazines within a few months of each other
run feature stories, illustrations in color, and even place
the lovely purple and green beauty of the African violet
upon their covers.

Not until the autumn of 1946, however, was there
any test of popularity. Then the H. G. Hastings Company in Atlanta, Georgia, sponsored the first African
Violet Show and the ensuing thousands of visiting
"violet" fans required the attention of the police to keep
traffic in hand.

But this was not the only time the police had to deal
with African violet furor. A correspondent writes of
what happened in one little Pennsylvania town: "It
seems someone had grown a violet there that was a dirty
white and some man—possibly a grower—propagated
and advertised it around as a yellow. Now he wishes he
had not. The people of Manheim have been nearly crazy
answering questions from collectors, in the state and out,
who have traveled miles to see the wonder and to buy a
plant or even just a leaf of it. Finally Manheim had to
refer the situation to the local magistrate. He posted
notices all around the town—THERE ARE NO YEL-
LOW VIOLETS HERE."

Discovery

The African violet is, of course, not a violet at all even
though it does come from Africa and its more usual deep
purple blooms are of violet form and color. Actually it is

a member of the Gesneria family to which belongs the velvet-leaved gloxinia. It was first discovered by Baron Walter von Saint Paul. His father, Hofmarschal Baron von Saint Paul of Fischbach in Silesia—president of the Dendrological Society of Germany, a group devoted to the study of trees—took particular interest in this botanical discovery.

Development

To the publisher of *Curtis Magazine*, that enchanting English publication which you can perhaps find in bound volumes among the horticultural books in your library, he wrote:

"The *Saintpaulia* was discovered by my son, who lives in East Africa where he owns plantations of vanilla and India-rubber trees. It was found in two localities; one about an hour from Tanga, in wooded places, in the fissures of limestone rocks, as well as in rich soil with plenty of vegetable matter. This place is not more than fifty to one hundred and fifty feet above the sea level. The second place is in the primeval forest of Numbara, likewise in shady situations, but on granite rocks, two thousand five hundred feet above the sea. It is much more plentiful in the former place. Several varieties have been discovered that differ slightly in color of the flowers but all are blue."

From seeds sent to England by Baron Walter, plants were raised by a Dr. Herman Wendland of Herrenhausen. When these flowered in 1893, he exhibited them in Ghent at the International Horticultural Exhibit and they "shared with Eulophiella exhibited by Messrs. Linden the honour of being the two most botanically interesting plants in the exhibition." The next year continental nurserymen carried the seed and the *Revue L'Horticulture Belge et Etrangere,* beside a picture of a rather unrealistic and very blue saintpaulia with very pink petal reverses, remarked *"Sa floraison est ininterrompue pendant tout d'hiver. . . . Elle sera promptement accuellie par tous les amateurs auxquels elle promet les plus vives jouissances aux époque de l'année où les fleurs sont les plus rares."* And plants of this marvelous subject blooming "in the time of year when flowers are rarest" were offered by L'Etablissement Ed. Pynaert-Van Geert for six francs each.

Flowering plants were also developed in the Royal Gardens of England. The procedure was that prescribed for the gloxinia. A half century later we still grow saintpaulia seeds the gloxinia way but the culture of the plant itself has many a green-thumb gardener puzzled. Perhaps because in its native state the African violet grows under such varying conditions as "rock fissures" and "rich soil," and at such different altitudes, in civilization it also offers contradictions. This results in one enthusiast's claiming success by methods quite opposite to those of another.

In Homes and Greenhouses

Yet success most certainly is achieved and even under rather makeshift conditions. Indeed, no one can dispute the possibilities of the African violet as a hobby plant for collectors. At least one hundred and seventy-five varieties appear by name in lists gathered throughout this country. Undoubtedly some duplication exists, although with my own eyes I have seen seventy-four *different* varieties. These were grown most handsomely in her small house by Elsie C. Freed in Feasterville, Pennsylvania. On her window sills at every exposure some two hundred plants always offer lovely color.

An acquaintance, Mrs. Paul Dissinger, in Lancaster, successfully propagates enough plants under home conditions to carry on locally a business involving the sale of five hundred plants yearly. In Bethayres, Anne Tinari, the wife of a nurseryman, began raising plants for her own interest and pleasure. Then under the pressure of friends, she commenced selling them. Today in two greenhouses, each sixteen by thirty-two feet, built just for her violets, she does a business of thousands of plants yearly.

Pansy Barnes, a doctor's wife in Shenandoah, Iowa, found in her growing African violet venture release from the anxieties of the war years. In time she began advertising and became so widely known that to her door came traveling enthusiasts from as far away as Long Island, New York, twelve hundred miles distant. Mrs. Barnes has even developed certain varieties of her own which, when propagated in sufficient quantity, will enrich the collections of enthusiasts East and West.

In California an invalid for ten years from arthritis writes, "I have found physical, mental, and spiritual comfort in my violets. I raise them only for my own pleasure, to give my friends, and other shut-ins. They help to satisfy that creative urge denied me in other mediums of expression."

In the South, Mrs. O. C. Williamson, the wife of a minister in Charlotte, North Carolina, turned her hobby into a serious business when her husband's activities were curtailed by illness. I know, too, one husband-and-wife team, the Orrells, who are such enthusiasts that they were willing one Washington's Birthday to travel from Maryland to Feasterville, Pennsylvania, over icy roads, not yet cleared by snow plows, just to sit in on a conference of other African violet fans! And so it goes via this pleasant violet path. Women everywhere enrich their lives, bear their burdens, broaden their interests, make new friends through corresponding with other enthusiasts and through visits to clubs, and even develop profitable businesses.

Wholesale commercial florists are also contributing to this attractive plant group. I have visited their collections from Pennsylvania to Oregon and I have discovered that when a grower once gets African violet fever, his feeling for other plants is quite likely to wane.

Saintpaulia Futures

What is needed now is an accurate system of classification, the organization of local societies for study and exchange, and further scientific investigation by qualified botanists. In Georgia, committees are codifying nomenclature and societies recently formed there are meeting for clarifying discussion. Round-robin groups associated with *Flower Grower* magazine are pooling information through the exchange of letters.

Some of the state universities have been studying the preferences of the African violet in order to pass on to amateurs a fairly basic set of cultural rules. For this is a temperamental subject. It quite readily offers years of continuous bloom to one amateur but only healthy leaves and not a spot of color to another. Indeed, to each of us who loves it the African violet is both challenge and delight.

CHAPTER TWO

Culturally Speaking

MANY PLANTS are grown for their foliage. Not so the African violet. Although without a single bud or blossom it is a handsome pot plant, flowers are the reward everyone seeks and the owner of a non-blooming specimen suffers frustration. The essential aim of culture therefore is flowers.

If a mature plant does not bloom, it is because some element of its condition is unsatisfactory. When there is a proper concatenation of circumstances, African violets bloom madly and to some degree throughout the year. The proud possessor of such plants may have just happened upon the pleasing formula or he may have proceeded purposely, carefully checking each aspect of culture as it is known to please this sometimes apparently stubborn house plant.

Place in Winter

First there is the selection of a site, an ideal location, for the growth of flowering plants. Since the native habitat of the African violet is "in wooded places" and "in the primeval forest . . . in shady situations" it is obvious that this is no plant to grow in a flood of sunshine. Indeed too much sunlight affects foliage adversely, turning it yellow, burning the margin of leaves, or causing malformation of leaf and flower. If only south windows are available, however, plants can be placed there with the brightness tempered by a glass curtain or a Venetian blind, the slats tilted upward during sunniest hours.

In fact, I have watched plants produce a fairly continuous procession of bloom in a small house where they were growing contentedly at every exposure. At light northern windows with no sunshine I have observed young plants of duPont Blue, a rather slow-growing variety, produce beautifully over a period of many months and in April, I have counted on each one ten and eleven open blossoms and innumerable buds.

Generally speaking, saintpaulias flower well in any light situation or in any sunny place where the brightness is somewhat diffused. The stronger the light, the deeper the color tones and the greater the floriferousness, within the limits of safety, of course. Light must also be tempered according to the season. A sunny eastern window without a curtain in January may suit your violets to a T but in April and September when daylight lasts longer and sunshine is stronger, a little shading is essential.

Place in Summer

Throughout the summer, indirect light suffices. Plants growing indoors from May to October flower freely in north windows which are kept open for long periods during each day. Or they may be set on a lightly shaded porch where pleasantly humid outdoor conditions increase their well-being and stimulate them to colorful performance. African violets are not house plants to be casually trusted to the open garden. Although in their native habitat saintpaulia species endure driving rain, the varieties of today, which have known the comforts of civilization, are not so tolerant. They require shelter. In protected locations, however, and with plenty of watering during summer dry spells, they bloom magnificently if sunk rim-deep in a garden bed, like other house plants. Although White Lady and Pink Beauty have produced very pale foliage under such outdoor conditions, my darker varieties, like Blue Girl, thrive and bloom amazingly. This is particularly true of very young plants.

Other enthusiasts sometimes forced by holiday plans to try summer plunging are so pleased by the results, they continue the practice year after year even without the necessity. One collector writes:

"My outdoor success, however, may be largely due to the ideal spot we prepared around our pool. The first summer of my African violet 'hobbying' we were faced with the vacation problem and there was little choice but to dig holes for the pots and trust that the elements and Mother Nature would be kind. The location, now selected each summer, has a northwestern exposure. It is heavily shaded by huge old oak trees and an underbrush of lacy ferns and other woodsy plant life. With the help of thorough soakings, which my good neighbor attends to during prolonged dry spells, my African violets invariably greet our return each August with a vivid carpet of blue."

Where it is necessary to leave African violets for a time to their own devices, a shaded spot out of the wind is best but some artificial watering is almost bound to be necessary for plunged plants. Of course it would be dangerous to depot them and plant them directly in a garden bed. By autumn, such plants would develop root systems which would be difficult to fit again into containers and repotting would necessitate much retarding root pruning.

Temperature and Ventilation

The best thing about these beautiful East African natives is their tolerance of the usual household heat. Too often delightful house plants, for bloom and survival, must be grown at less than sixty degrees, an uncomfortable state for humans. The African violet is a plant which thrives in an atmosphere even up to seventy-five degrees F. with the ideal temperature seventy to seventy-two degrees. A temperature of less than sixty degrees checks both growth and flowering.

A fresh atmosphere is essential. Even in cold weather closeness is detrimental but cool air must never blow *directly* on the plants. Indirect ventilation from an adjoining room is the safest plan. In most dwellings where doors to the outside are frequently in use the matter of fresh air takes care of itself. Only in the greenhouse does ventilation become part of a program.

Watering

Method of watering and temperature of water have much to do with success, although plants watered in different ways may bloom equally well. As a triumphant record here is an account sent to me in 1943. "I have an African violet, four and one-half years old. It has been repotted but once. Yet in that time, it has bloomed continuously, sometimes with twenty flowers and never with less than five blossoms at any time, winter or summer, even when it was being repotted. I allow the plant to get fairly dry, then water thoroughly by setting the pot into a pan of water overnight. Again it is allowed to dry out fairly well before the soaking process is repeated. I pinch off the bottom leaves as they ripen or turn yellow."

Some amateurs also report excellent flowering from plants placed every other day in deep vessels of *hot* water. They remain until the water cools. Care is taken not to permit the water to reach the leaves or to wash over the rim of the pot.

Since the size and type of the pot, the weather, the season, the temperature, and the amount of sunshine are also factors affecting the amount of water needed, it may be that quite opposite practices will succeed under varying conditions.

I have known plants to bloom long and well which were grown in flat pots or azalea pans with a *constant* inch of water maintained in the pot saucer. Beginners will perhaps do best to follow Mrs. Freed's successful program:

"Mine are given a drink every morning, early. The soil is *never* allowed to become dry on top, but remains soft and crumbly to the touch. Occasionally a bit of mold appears as warning to give a little less water but this mold never seems to have been harmful and I consider it entirely different from a mold resulting from sour soil. Two or three times a year I very gently loosen the surface earth with a fork. This breaks the crust which forms from the heat of the sun and radiation. My plants are always watered from the saucer and never given more water than can be absorbed by early afternoon. The water is near room temperature but I do not bother to check it with a thermometer. I am of the opinion that with proper watering more and larger flowers are produced."

W. D. Holley gives this advice based on trials made on the African violet by twenty-six cooperating Connecticut women over a period of eighteen months:

"The African violet is not a cactus plant. To be successful it should have all the water it can use. The entire ball of soil should be soaked thoroughly at each watering, but to avoid danger from overwatering, water only when the top of the soil is slightly dry to the touch. It may not require daily watering but it does require daily checking. Severe drying seriously limits flowering."

Certainly it is easier to water saintpaulias thoroughly from below than from above since the leafy crown is

thick and the surface area for absorption is limited by
the broad spread of the foliage over the top and sometimes down over the sides of the pot as well. But top or
bottom watering is a matter of convenience not necessity. Water on the leaves will not harm them if they are
shaded until the hairy foliage dries and *if the water is of
room temperature.* This is most important. Even in
watering the soil, when leaves remain dry, warm rather
than cold water should be used as a health measure.

One fairly certain way of giving saintpaulias the
proper amount of moisture is to use "wicks" which draw
water from some vessel to the soil automatically. Wicks
operate on the principle of the coal oil lamp with water
substituted for oil. The best wicks, which are obtainable
from seed houses, are made of woven glass fiber or as-
bestos about one-fourth to one-half inch in diameter and
three to six inches long. A lamp wick can also be used
but only temporarily.

Attach the wick to the soil by first removing the plant
and the drainage material. Then push the wick through
the drainage hole of the empty pot. Unravel the wick a
little so that the fibers can be spread out over the bottom
of the pot on the inside and pack a little sand or soil over
them to keep them in place. Next put the plant back
securely and water the soil sufficiently for the wick to
drip water.

To supply the wick constantly with water, use a glass
jar or pottery flowerpot as a water-holding vessel. It
must be of a size to fit the flowerpot so tightly that it
supports it up to the rim, thus holding the plant well

above the bottom of the outside container. The wick hangs down into this lower area where a constant supply of water is maintained for the plant to draw on and relay to the soil as it is needed. If the outside container should become empty and the soil in consequence go dry, it will be necessary to thoroughly soak the soil surface from above before the water from below is replenished. Only in this way will absorption again be in operation.

Cleansing of Foliage

With precautions of light and temperature observed, occasional top syringing will tend to be refreshing and beneficial, cleansing foliage of dust and stimulating new growth. In greenhouses syringing with the hose is routine and many a housewife with glorious violets gives them a light Saturday morning shower "whether they need it or not" with a rubber sprayer attached to the faucet at the kitchen sink. Do not be afraid this procedure will cause leaf spot. At Ohio State University the reason for that unattractive foliage condition was discovered by the Department of Horticulture. This is the report of their saintpaulia experiment:

"The plants were grown in a low light intensity about four hundred to six hundred foot candles in the usual commercial manner. When either ice or bits of cold metal or glass objects were placed on the leaf, spotting developed in about twenty-four to forty-eight hours. Of course, the same type of spotting occurred if the water temperature was ten degrees lower than the house temperature. To illustrate, African violets are generally grown [in the greenhouse] at sixty degrees night temperature and if water at fifty degrees was splashed on the leaf, spotting would develop within three days. In one experiment, the African violets were placed in a refrigerator at fifty degrees and water at fifty degrees was splashed on them after the plants were uniformly cool. No spotting developed under these conditions.

"The conclusions of this work was that if cold water was used, it should never be splashed on the foliage, but instead should be applied directly to the soil. The most satisfactory method, of course, is to use water at the same temperature at which the plant is grown."

Humidity

A very dry atmosphere, particularly if it is hot, is not at all desirable for saintpaulias, yet with most modern heating systems it is difficult to maintain a humid condition of air. When many plants are grown together humidity is, of course, increased. Pans of water set on radiators or on a table also help by providing a constant source of evaporation. This device is particularly helpful with hot air systems of heating.

Many of us have found too that African violets thrive and bloom more freely if each plant is set on a pebble-filled saucer with some water always in it as a ready means of humidifying the surrounding air. According to our convictions then, we keep the supply of water high enough for the pot just to rest *in* it or low enough for the pot just to rest *above* it. Damp sand in the saucers or tray which contain the pots has proved another good growing device.

In a terrarium or in an aquarium or battery jar, with a pane of glass placed over the opening, most pleasant and humid conditions can be constantly maintained but it is important to keep such plantings out of the sun or they will be far too hot. It is also necessary each day to raise the glass at the top and ventilate the plants for a few minutes. Very attractive groups can be arranged for such glassed-in plantings. Particularly charming are purple African violets, wax begonias, Pink Pearl, and the delicate maidenhair ferns, which are likewise dependent on humidity. Only if these glass gardens are kept too wet will there be signs of decay. With so little moisture escaping, almost no watering is required.

Brief Guidance

Here then is a six-point program which, faithfully followed, is known to produce fairly constant bloom on saintpaulias:

1. In winter, place plants preferably at east or north windows. Avoid strong sunlight.

2. In summer, place plants at north windows, kept open for long daily periods, or on a lightly shaded porch.

3. Maintain a house temperature of seventy to seventy-two degrees with no more than a ten-degree drop at night.

4. Maintain a fresh atmosphere but in avoiding closeness be mindful of the dangers of chilling.

5. Water from the saucer with room-temperature water. Apply enough each morning to be absorbed by afternoon.

6. Make special provisions for humidity if the air in the house is noticeably dry or if temperatures incline to rise much above seventy degrees.

CHAPTER THREE

Down to Earth

MANY CONTRADICTORY statements have been made as to the proper soil for saintpaulias. Avoid a heavy clay soil, is the definite dictum of one hobbyist; a light soil is unnecessary, claims a large commercial grower who is experimenting with clay plus peat moss and a very little sand. Keep the soil sweet, one collector advises, since the African violet is native to localities of limestone. Likewise with history in view, one wholesaler is making extensive experiments with basic slag. Another is advising the addition of a little powdered charcoal to each potful of soil to offset the acidity induced by constant watering and the use in growing mixtures of peat moss and leaf mold.

Undoubtedly this is a case where there is "much to be said on both sides" or perhaps I should put it, on all sides, since there are certainly more than two opinions. It will be interesting to hear the results of the basic-slag experiments, for in view of natural habitat, they should prove affinity. Some of Mrs. Freed's experiences would also indicate such a correlation. She has had better results when she used soil scraped up from beneath a cherry tree, where one would expect it to be sweet, than from soil from under an oak, where undoubtedly it was acid.

It may be we will finally come to the conclusion that the saintpaulia is one of those plants of amenable disposition which grows well in neutral, or slightly sweet, or slightly acid mediums. Considering its fine root system, I cannot imagine its doing well in a very heavy soil mixture and from what I have observed at my own window and in the collections of friends, a light, easily penetrated soil mixture seems a pretty safe choice.

Certainly degree of acidity influences color of flower and foliage, even if it does not affect health. Acidity brings out redness in leaves and deepens the blueness of blossoms, just as it does so obviously with hydrangeas which turn from pink to blue when grown in acid soil. Mrs. Barnes observed that "Supreme when grown in California and kept on gravel had green foliage. In Iowa on peat moss the backs of the leaves were all red. However, *plants bloomed beautifully* under both conditions."

Ferne Kellar's experience in Des Moines seems to bear out the contention that alkalinity, or sweetness, is a saintpaulia preference. She writes: "I cannot grow African violets in acid soil. I have tried it, using a soil tester to determine degree of acidity. Saintpaulias were not discovered growing in acid soil. I prefer soil to test 7 pH, that is neutral. A little variation either way is all right but not to the extent of 6 pH or 6.5 pH, as some growers claim, not with our rich soil anyway."

A Soil Formula

This is Mrs. Kellar's preferred soil formula:
  3 parts good black soil (gumbo)
  1 part peat
  1 part compost (about half manure)
  1 part rotted manure
  2 parts sand
She adds to each bushel of this soil mixture:
  1 six-inch potful of superphosphate
  1 gallon of wood ashes containing bits of burnt wood or charcoal

Her formula might be considered a specialist's mixture, fine for those who are willing to devote much time and care to their saintpaulias. As an amateur collector, you may well respect Mrs. Kellar's advice and yet proceed on a simpler schedule with every expectation of growing handsome plants.

Potting

When you get plants from the florist they will be tightly potted in three- or four-inch pots with a close multiple-crowned top festive with bloom. You can if you wish continue to grow African violets in this way, shifting them on to a size larger pot as blooming dwindles a little and an examination of roots indicates a somewhat pot-bound condition. A far handsomer plant will develop, however, if when the need for the first shift arises, you transfer the plant to a five-inch pan, bulb, or azalea pot, as those shallow flowerpots are called.

You can either separate the crown then, spacing several sections of it in the new pan and reserving others for separate potting, or you can shift the plant on, as it is, and let it spread out of its own accord. (The latter is far safer procedure.) In either case the greater surface space will permit the development of the excellent foliage to the fullest extent. Leaves will extend and droop over the edge of the pot and *bloom from an open crown will be even freer* than in the more narrowly potted specimen.

This liberal system of potting is contrary to general pot-plant practice, but in the case of the African violet plenty of root room seems to increase rather than to retard flowering. Furthermore, plants started at home and generously potted from the two-inch pot stage on appear to me to better advantage at every point than commercially grown specimens. These are necessarily restricted to small containers to save greenhouse space.

There are, however, two schools of thought on this. Alma Wright, whose handsome plants form an extensive collection, finds that with weekly feedings and frequent watering saintpaulias will grow well and bloom constantly in very small pots. If you have little room for your violet collection or must use quite small containers to fit the narrow glass shelves of a window garden, the small-pot system may prove more satisfactory for you.

Fertilizer

Little extra fertilizer, or even none at all, will be necessary if plenty of leaf mold has been used in the original potting soil. Equal thirds of peat moss or leaf mold, sand, and loam is a general pot-plant formula which also seems to apply to saintpaulias. The fine roots find a comfortable medium in such a loose porous base and since the plants are not rapid growers, the quick-acting fertilizers often prove detrimental. The addition, however, of quite *small* amounts of plant food seems to improve foliage tone and to increase the number and size of flowers.

With the regular potting mixture, and good cultural conditions, succession of bloom is fairly well assured. Quality of blossoms but not necessarily number may improve with the extra food, although I have seen very handsome, long-flowering African violets which received no extra plant food. They seemed to be adequately nourished by the fresh, rich leaf mold liberally supplied by an adequate potting program.

Certainly it does no harm to give supplementary feedings after an extended period of heavy growth and free flowering. I always believe, however, in letting plants at such a stage have a well-earned rest of a few weeks. This seems to me just plain common-sense procedure, especially for late spring or early summer after the height of the saintpaulia season.

Then I believe in following the advice of the Missouri Botanical Garden, "to use about one teaspoonful of a complete fertilizer to a quart of water and apply this mixture as a regular watering once every week or two."

Plant tablets are such a convenient form of food that I have sometimes used them, according to the manufacturer's directions, or else dissolved five tablets in a four-ounce glass of water to make a stock solution and applied a teaspoonful of this liquid to the surface soil of each four- or five-inch pot plant once every other week. (Such practice plus repotting in a fresh soil rich in humus usually revitalizes ailing plants often brought to me for resurrection.) Dissolved horticultural vitamin B^1 tablets are good conditioners for saintpaulias, as Charles J. Hudson, Jr., has suggested, but they are not meant, of course, to take the place of fertilizer only to help a plant to that state of health where it can beneficially use fertilizer.

A correspondent from Berkeley writes of excellent results from the Plant Chem products. Her scheme of culture seems to indicate an acidity preference. She writes that as an invalid with arthritis she has found that African violets "help to satisfy that creative urge denied me in other mediums of expression." We active gardeners who also love these friendly saintpaulias can well understand this Californian woman's delight in these essentially responsive subjects. She reports that one of her eight-year-old plants has carried as many as forty blooms and concludes, "I use a cupful (standard strength) once a month, sub-irrigation, of acid Plant Chem Salts and the same amount each of the other three weeks of regular Plant Chem Salts. I also add a teaspoonful of Plant Chem solution (both regular and acid) to each eight-ounce glass containing leaves which I am propagating."

Also from the West Coast comes a nutrient solution

in which some experimenters claim plants grow better than in soil. I have no personal knowledge of these experiments but have been much interested in the results obtained by Claude Gortatowsky who in Atlanta, Georgia, has been applying hydroponics to saintpaulias and using this nutrient solution from the University of California.

He reports: "Varieties of violets cultivated included Sailor Boy, Viking, Amethyst, Mrs. William K. duPont, Norseman, and others. A bed of coarse sand was used as the retaining medium. The formula contained salts of nitrogen, phosphorus, potash, calcium, magnesium, sulphur; also iron, manganese, boron, zinc, copper, molybdenum as trace elements. Acidity of the solution was adjusted to a pH of 5 by addition of several drops of two and one-half per cent sulphuric acid per gallon.

"Leaf cuttings are placed in the sand bed as customary and watered with the nutrient solution twice a week, the first watering begun at once. Each four to six weeks the sand bed is flushed out thoroughly with water.

"The cuttings root in a normal manner; growth of the plants is vigorous with an extensive root system spreading laterally rather than extending in depth. Flowering is prolific and plants thus grown were never found to have contracted any of the violet diseases.

"It is possible to transplant from the sand bed to soil. Plants that have been grown in soil, however, do not thrive so well on being transferred to the nutrient solution and sand method of culture."

Every saintpaulia enthusiast eventually develops his own preference for soils and fertilizers. If the method you have followed to date has given you a saintpaulia crop of satisfactory size and duration, go right along the way you have been. If you have been meeting with disappointments, try one of these programs suggested by other more successful hobbyists or commercial growers.

CHAPTER FOUR

From Leaf to Plant

SAINTPAULIAS are responsive plants to propagate. Indeed their popularity is partially due to the ease of extending a collection or of increasing the number of plants of some appealing variety. Through the neighborly exchange of leaves or the reciprocal mailing of them to unmet but not unknown distant "violet friends" almost every desired variety may be acquired and the windows of a house soon filled with oncoming youngsters.

Saintpaulias lend themselves readily to increase through division, or through leaf propagation, in which both soil and water methods prove practical. If you have a mature specimen with a thick crown you can *with care* separate it into a number of smaller individual plants. Just remove the pot and very gently pull the sections of the plant apart. Several single divisions will readily appear, but some may cling together in small clumps of two or three. You can pot these as they are or take the chance, not always successful, of cutting them apart with a sharp knife and then potting them separately.

Three-inch-diameter pots or the smallest sized pan

will not be too large for most of the divisions. With plenty of surface room they will soon develop their large handsome leaves to the fullest and maintain an open crown from which an almost constant procession of flowering stems will push forth. Use the same soil as before—equal thirds of sand, loam, and leaf mold or humus—or use leaf mold alone, if that is easier for you.

Many persons are also using Vermiculite, a mica product which comes by the bag. The coarser particles they find best for the potting mixture, the finer part for rooting, and the finest for planting seeds. If Vermiculite is pressed through a quarter-inch mesh screen it readily separates into material of different degrees of coarseness. The majority who have used this medium consider it a preventative of crown rot, and find that it aids the germination of seeds and the development of the plant.

Very fine plants can also be grown from mature leaves cut with stems or petioles from parent plants. These rooted in water or in a sandy soil mixture develop into flowering-sized plants in about eight to nine months, rarely in six, but the length of time depends on cultural conditions and also on the nature of the variety being propagated. Sometimes within a year such plants are large enough for division. So all you really need to satisfy even an unlimited enthusiasm for African violets is a few leaves from plants of the varieties you admire and, of course, considerable patience.

Such a formula holds except for Pink Beauty, Blue Girl, and White Lady. These varieties are protected by plant patent and you may not propagate them without permission. *If you are a commercial grower* and wish to handle these three patented varieties, you may obtain a propagating license by applying to the following firms: to Ulery Greenhouses, 1325 Maiden Lane, Springfield, Ohio, for Blue Girl; to Fred C. Gloeckner and Company, Inc., 15 East 26th Street, New York 10, New York, for White Lady; and to Holton and Hunkel Company, 797 N. Milwaukee Street, Milwaukee 1, Wisconsin, for Pink Beauty. Permission involves the signing of a contract with the owners and arrangements to buy plant labels for a stated fee per hundred. These labels bear the name of the plant and its patent number. You are required to place a label on every plant you sell of a patented variety.

Patents for propagating rights for Gorgeous and Pink Girl have now been granted to R. G. Baxter of Youngstown, Ohio. At present Mr. Baxter plans to control these rights himself and not to grant permits to other growers.

Rooting Leaves in Water

Now here are two practical methods developed for leaf propagating by home gardeners. Cover a water-filled glass tumbler with wax paper held in place with a rubber band. Pierce the paper in three places. Insert the leaf stems in these holes and deeply enough for the stems to reach into the water. Set the glass in a fully light but not sunny window. If you use faucet rather than rain water, let it stand uncovered for twenty-four hours beforehand so that all chlorine may be released.

It is also possible to work even more simply. In a

shallow glass dish or soup bowl a number of different varieties can easily be started. Just fill the dish with enough small rounded stones to support the leaf stems, and maintain a sufficient supply of water to keep the ends of the stems moist.

In two to four weeks, depending on variety and location, roots will appear at the ends of the stems. Change the water then. By the end of another week or so a small green leaf may appear at the base of each parent leaf. If the parent leaf has begun to deteriorate, you can now make a transfer of rooted leaves to three-inch pots of light soil or pure sand. If the parent leaf remains firm and healthy, wait until a cluster of leaves about one inch long appears.

To make the transfer from water to soil with the least possible danger and best possible results to the developing plant, follow the system which Dorothy Reynolds suggests: "Use a small custard cup containing a small amount of water. Place the rooted leaf in the vessel, spreading the roots. Sift fine soil around them until all the water has been absorbed. Then both the soil and leaf may be lifted out with the aid of a spoon."

The time of propagation varies, of course. Ionantha leaves root very quickly, I notice, while the duPont varieties certainly take their time. No leaves can be depended upon to produce roots very promptly but so long as the parent leaf remains healthy and does not soften and decay, the growth of roots and new leaves will eventually occur. Sometimes it actually takes months.

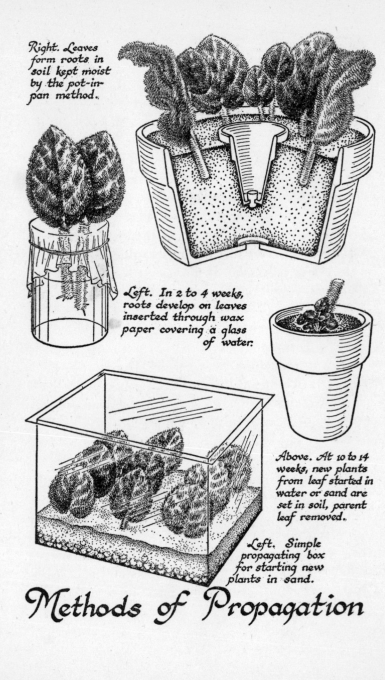

Right. Leaves form roots in soil kept moist by the pot-in-pan method.

Left. In 2 to 4 weeks, roots develop on leaves inserted through wax paper covering a glass of water.

Above. At 10 to 14 weeks, new plants from leaf started in water or sand are set in soil, parent leaf removed.

Left. Simple propagating box for starting new plants in sand.

Methods of Propagation

Left. Blue Boy leaf at 10 weeks; leaf with stem may produce three successive crops.

Right. Stemless leaf of Viking at 10 weeks; root systems not so developed but may produce more small plants.

Right. Leaves of several varieties develop roots in a flat dish of small supporting stones and water.

Below. Plants started from leaves at the 4½-to-5 months stage.

Above. A 4½-to-5-months plant, well-rooted, usually blooms in 8 to 9 months.

Methods of Propagation

When quite a cluster of new leaves appears, cut the parent leaf away. Remove it sooner if it shows signs of deterioration but often it is not necessary to discard it for a long time. If a variety is scarce or your supply limited, you may be able to grow a second or even a third crop of saintpaulias from the same treasured leaf. Each time you will, of course, be working with a shorter, sharply cut petiole until a third planting is made perhaps with no petiole at all and only the leaf base to insert in the soil. Even so, you can expect success as many have found from experience that the same leaf will produce as fine a third crop as it did a first. This is particularly true of duPont Lavender Pink which being a slow and valuable grower is always cherished down to the last leaf.

Expect some little setback at the time of the water-to-soil transfer while roots are adjusting to the new medium. In less than five months, however, you will have a well-established, thrifty plant which should in less than a year produce flowers.

Rooting Leaves in Soil

A second method has been developed by enthusiasts who prefer to start their plants in soil. They have found that battery jars, terrariums, and aquariums are excellent makeshift greenhouses for propagating.

Over the bottom of a fish bowl or other suitable receptacle spread an inch of pebbles. Cover the small stones with two inches of fine sandy soil moistened well but not made soggy. Then insert the violet leaves just deeply enough for them to escape the soil surface. If they rest on it, decay often starts. (In experiments at the Missouri Botanical Garden, however, Saintpaulia, Blue Boy, in the case of two plants out of many hundreds, showed viviparous characteristics with "plantlets developing directly on the leaf blade" when the base of the leaf and not the end of the petiole was in direct contact with the growing medium.)

Firm the soil mixture well around each stem. Set the aquarium in a light but not sunny place. Over the top stretch a kitchen bowl cover or else a piece of cellophane secured by a rubber band.

Little attention will now be needed for several weeks. The first few days after planting inspect the soil to be sure you moistened it well enough at the start for it to stay damp. If moisture collect on the sides of the glass, remove the cover long enough to wipe away the excess. In a not too warm and not sunny place such attention will hardly be necessary. In four to six weeks the rooted leaves will be at the new-plant stage and ready for separate potting. Those who have followed this plan report bloom on new plants in six months.

Pot-in-Pan Method

Then there is the pot-in-pan method. Use moist sand or sand and peat moss for a rooting mixture. Fill a large porous bulb pan with this and into the center insert a small stoppered flowerpot. Keep the small center pot filled with water. The amount of water will decrease because of slow seepage through the walls of the inner pot. This seepage provides the surrounding soil area with adequate and even moisture. Insert the leaf stems in the soil at a slight angle, the upper surfaces to the front. In two to four weeks roots will form and in the course of another month new sprouts will push up to the surface. In three months' time well-developed plants will form and be ready for separate potting.

Any one of these methods—water glass, aquarium, pot-in-pan—or your own variation of them, will start a violet collection for you or increase the valued number already in hand.

Two experimenters report they have used Rootone to advantage and with it developed flowering plants in a four-months period. Others report that root-growing substances are of little value with saintpaulias. In any case, rooting and flowering seem to be hastened by a spring rather than an autumn start. Some amateurs, indeed, have reported late September flowering from early May propagating. Perhaps the former idea that leaf-to-blossom took a year was based on autumn and winter propagating. Even so, flowering in less than eight months is fairly unusual.

CHAPTER FIVE

With Seed and Cross

AFRICAN VIOLETS can also be raised from seed as many hobbyists have found to their amusement and delight. From a single seed pod it is possible to obtain as many different varieties as one gets seeds. Only don't consider that each seedling represents a brand new African violet.

Already the saintpaulia clan in its mere fifty years of development is suffering from a bad case of duplication. If after careful comparison of your outstanding seedling plant with similar named varieties and perhaps also with the notable unnamed seedlings of other collectors, you are convinced—and they are convinced—that you have something new and different, then go ahead and name your plant. Register the new name and a detailed description of the variety with the African Violet Society of America (2694 Lenox Road N.E., Atlanta, Georgia) and share it by generously propagating it. But please do not confuse the issue by naming and propagating ahead of thorough investigation.

Incidentally in the matter of names, may I make a plea for nomenclature that is descriptive and individual. As a gardener who enjoys many kinds of plants and likes to be familiar with their names without making an encyclopedia of my mind, I resent cross-reference naming which results in the carnation-flowered marigold, the peony-type rose, and the rosebud geranium. In selecting new saintpaulia names let's make them belong like White Lady, Pink Beauty, and Blue Girl. I like the duPont and Supreme classifications which name the strain and then define the color and I feel sure we are all grateful for the simplicity of Saintpaulia, Blushing Maiden, which gives us an idea of what to expect from the plant so named.

If you grow plants from the dustlike seed you may or may not consider the process more tedious than propagation from leaves. You will undoubtedly be surprised to discover, as I was, that flowers appear quite as soon on seedlings as on leaf-grown plants, sometimes sooner. Very likely your plants have not formed seed. If they have, it is pure accident since specimens grown indoors are not subject to the visitations of insects which are the usual and, in most cases, necessary means of transfer of pollen from one flower to another. However, you yourself can do the trick artificially and with a soft paintbrush transfer pollen from one of the flowers you have selected for parenthood to the other.

Parents by Selection

And it is wise to select rather than to take a lot of trouble and achieve only an inferior lot of seedlings because they were developed from poor-quality parents. Since the duPont strain is definitely superior, if you like its characteristics, you might choose duPont Blue with its sturdy fluted leaf and large dark flower for one parent and perhaps the excellent Neptune, also fine of leaf and flower, for the other. Mrs. Kellar obtained bloom in six to seven months from such a well-chosen cross. Or you might work for doubleness, selecting parents with additional petals, or try for paler blues by crossing a lavender with a white. Only don't work for yellows and produce only soiled-laundry whites!

Saintpaulia Botany

An understanding of the botanical elements involved in cross-fertilization is essential. The saintpaulia produces bisexual flowers, that is, each one contains both male and female organs. Examine a flower and you will discover that it has four distinct parts. Use a magnifying glass or hand lens to see them more clearly. You will notice sepals, petals, stamen with anthers, and pistil with stigma.

The five sepals are those green enfolding parts at the back of the flowers. They form a protective envelope for the developing bud and later for the seed pod.

Petals are easily discerned. They give the saintpaulias their color—purple, pink, or white.

The stamen represents the male element of the flower. It consists of slender yellow filaments terminating in pollen sacks or anthers. The saintpaulia has four anthers and two are fertile, two sterile. Inside the fertile anthers grains of pollen develop.

The pistil is the female element. It is the noticeably

different structure you see coming out of the center of the flower. It consists of three quite readily distinguishable parts. Low down at its base is a slight enlargement in which are held the immature seeds or ovules awaiting fertilization. This swelling elongates into a slender column called the style, which terminates in a tiny disklike structure, known as the stigma. This becomes sticky after a flower has been open for a few days and continues so for several hours after the blossoms fall. During this quite long interval in the plant's development the stigma is in proper condition to retain grains of pollen on its sticky surface, if you transfer them there through a process known as hand-pollination.

Pollination

Pollination is a term describing the reception and retention of pollen by the stigma. When a cross "takes" the ovary or seed pod at the base of the pistil begins to enlarge and finally to project beyond the protecting sepals. It requires from six to nine months for the fertilized seed to mature and ripen sufficiently for sowing. Spring pollination usually produces seed in about six months while summer and autumn pollination requires eight to nine months.

Commercial growers usually effect pollination by removing, if possible, even before the bud opens, unwanted pollen-bearing anthers from the female parent so as to avoid self-fertilization. Then they transfer pollen from the anther of the chosen male parent to the stigma of the female by means of a small paintbrush. The amateur may be able to pollinate simply by rubbing the anther of one flower against the stigma of another during the period when the stigma is sticky. Mrs. W. H. Odom who has been most successful in inducing saintpaulias to set seed, describes a method of her own:

"It may be necessary to bruise the anthers in order to release some of the pollen contained inside. My favorite and most successful method of pollinating has been to cut away a small portion of the anther with a sharp pair of small scissors thus preparing an opening to the pollen. A fine camel's-hair brush may be used to transplant the pollen from the anther to the pistil but I prefer to insert the pistil of another flower in the tiny opening which has been cut in the anther. In this way the pistil comes in direct contact with the freshly exposed pollen and the style of the pistil immediately becomes yellow with grains of pollen."

Mrs. Odom also believes that a seed-bearing parent is the better for some special care. She finds that plants ripen seed sooner if they are kept a little on the dry side and that they "often require extra nutrients while seed pods are maturing. If proper nutrient is furnished, a well-matured, healthy plant should suffer no ill effects from growing a few seed pods. Blossoms may be quite scarce during this period. In fact, I do not recommend letting a plant, which is striving to produce two or more seed pods, come into full blossom. The buds may be pinched out as soon as they appear."

Seed Sowing

Next comes the question of the proper time to sow. Some growers believe in sowing as soon as seeds ripen. Others, of whom Fay Wilcox is one, believe that seed gains in vitality if after being gathered, it is allowed one to two months for further maturing and drying.

In one of her experiments she planted seed collected in September on November twenty-sixth. Germination occurred December twenty-fourth. Then came a long period in which the planting apparently stood still with no further top growth appearing. Evidently the business of rooting was underway for early in February seedlings had developed sufficiently to be just large enough to handle. With a toothpick they were pricked out and planted at two-inch distances in a flat of leaf mold.

Once you have acquired ripe seed, your new crop is in sight, although the dust-fine product makes belief in miracles essential. However, the germ of life does lie in those infinitesimal particles, as you soon will discover. Sow the seed on the surface of a pan of light, sandy soil. Cover with only a slight sifting of sand, firm with a brick or piece of wood, or with the flat of your hand. Then place a piece of glass over the sowing until seedlings appear. Water from below to maintain a constantly moist condition. Keep the pan in a warm, light place. Plant the seedlings in separate pots, two inches in diameter, when they are large enough to handle. Use for the first potting of seedings either pure leaf mold or whatever soil mixture you have successfully used for your larger plants.

Hand-pollination to bloom is a long process. To the patient hobbyist, collector, or hybridizer, improvement-bent, it is a fascinating sequence of events. The casual grower of saintpaulias whose interest is only in colorful flowers for the window should not even attempt it. It is fun though, if you have the time and interest to do it.

CHAPTER SIX

Companions, Corsages, and Arrangements

ALTHOUGH THE ardent saintpaulia fan and collector is usually blind to all other house plants, there are less devout followers who enjoy growing other things too. In a window garden or on a sheltered open porch they find that saintpaulias may be grown in attractive association with various other pot plants having approximately the same requirements of light and heat. Ferns look well with African violets and, of course, such vines as philodendron, pothos, and grape ivy. These furnish an attractive green foil to the bright saintpaulia flowers, while their trailing or climbing habits make possible interesting compositions in a window or on a plant stand, set perhaps against the house wall of a porch.

Then there are certain flowering plants which are charming with "violets." The patience plant is one. I believe this was the first house plant I had as a child and today I find its obliging nature and continuous flowering, winter and summer, just as appealing as I did years ago. And it is so easy to grow in the same north or east window the saintpaulias prefer and so pretty there if salmon, pink, or red varieties are combined with the blue violets, or white ones with the pink saintpaulias.

Usually patience plants are not to be found at the florist since neighbors for generations have been passing around slips. A sharply cut or broken branch always has the easy makings of a new plant. In fact, it can be started along with a saintpaulia in the same glass of water.

Patience Plants

With ample quarters for pot plants, it may be you will enjoy collecting patience plants as well as saintpaulias. If you have a greenhouse, you will soon discover the suitability of the botanical name, Impatiens. This well describes the eagerness of the plant to sow seed as well as the speed of seedlings in producing flowers.

I once observed in a greenhouse a particularly floriferous group of impatiens whose progeny, self-sown, were coming into flower five and eight feet away. No inadvertent mixing of seeds with potting soil could explain the phenomenon since the distant seedlings appeared in the ashes around other plants and in the clean sand of the propagation bench, as well as on the surface soil of large and distant pot plants. Evidently the slight pressure of occasional overhead watering on seed cases was responsible for the far-away sowings. These were commencing to flower in January from seeding which must have taken place sometime after early September, when the parent plants had been brought inside.

From such indiscriminate sowings many shades and various types of plants result. You will find these, as well as plants from a sowing of mixed seeds, of more or less desirability. When you make cuttings, of course, you can select according to color and use. These can be of the common species, Impatiens sultani, which grows fifteen inches or so tall with green leaves and red flowers (nice with white "violets") or of one of the sultani hybrids or sports which appear in a white, blush, and pink to purple range.

Impatiens holsti grows somewhat taller than I. sultani. Its foliage is striped red and the larger flowers are a rich bright scarlet. There is also I. oliveri with exquisite lavender flowers over two inches across and rather like the bloom of myrtle. Oliveri is amenable to house culture and most lovely for a window garden featuring pink violets.

In collecting, you will discover impatiens specimens of considerable variability. In one group I saw some thirty-inch plants with turkey red flowers and green leaves. Others had dark foliage and either brick red or magenta flowers. I also saw plants not so tall with white flowers and one white with a red eye. A very spreading twelve-inch high plant bore brilliant pink flowers and striped leaves, while a glowing salmon spread twelve inches across but was less than six inches tall. With Saintpaulia, Blue Boy, it looked charming. These dwarf types are particularly attractive as bracket plants or as pot plants with violets on broad window sills.

Three- to four-inch impatiens cuttings taken in spring will commence to flower long before roots are properly developed. To conserve strength, pinch out the first buds. In two weeks cuttings are ready for two-inch pots. In another ten days they can be shifted to three's, and given a pinch of bone meal or of a complete plant food. Growers actually find them of salable size in a month! Cuttings made in fall are a little slower to root but even at that season a broken piece of patience plant will root readily if placed in a glass of water. If you use faucet rather than rain water, let it stand uncovered for twenty-four hours beforehand so that all chlorine may be released. Cuttings inserted in sand will root more quickly and also develop better. Tall varieties destined for the window garden require more pinching back than naturally low growers.

All patience plants are easy to keep in health. With so large a leaf area to transpire moisture, they are, though, noticeably thirsty. Indeed they dry out so quickly that a large pot plant in bright weather sometimes needs watering more than once a day. No excess moisture should be left standing in the saucer once the soil has been well saturated.

The patience plant thrives in any light window but blooms more freely with some eastern sunshine. Trim plants back a little in late spring to keep them shapely. Then place them on the porch on a stand or bench with your saintpaulias or plunge them in partial shade in the garden where they will round out a fine year-round performance by continuing to bloom all summer too.

Wax Begonias

Saintpaulia enthusiasts have also found begonias good companions, although fervor for two such extensive plant groups takes up tremendous space and spreads so far that

the family is likely to find itself living in the halls only.
A few wax begonias, however, are very pleasing among
saintpaulias, their upright growth and shining foliage of-
fering agreeable contrast.

Cuttings or seeds may be handled in the same way as
the African violets. Mature plants thrive under the same
conditions of light, but will do well in the cooler locations
at a window. Apparently untroubled by pest or disease,
the wax begonia flowers freely from October to June,
provided it is pinched back enough to keep it stocky and
branching and provided also it is neither overwatered nor
allowed to stand in water. If permitted to dry out well
between drinks and if the foliage is lightly cleansed once
a month, it will thrive. Unlike the saintpaulia it blooms
better if rather closely potted. The same soil mixture is
pleasing.

Gloxinias

A close relative of the saintpaulia, the gloxinia, is too
spreading a plant to be freely used with it unless there is
unlimited room. Admirers of the one, however, also find
the other appealing and since the same conditions are
agreeable, gloxinias are here suggested as a companion
crop. They have the advantage of summer flowering too
when saintpaulias are sometimes in a quiet and all-green
mood.

The velvet texture and rich, brilliant tones of gloxinias
are indeed a delight. If tubers are potted in February,
first blossoms will open early in June. Thereafter a charming succession is assured if a potful or two is started once

every two weeks until May. An autumn crop is readily obtained from seeds sown before the middle of March. As a rule, flowers appear in a little over four months from mature tubers and in a little over five months from seed.

Tubers may be purchased in mixture or in named varieties. When I am buying new ones, I select according to the colors of the large saintpaulias which are also destined to decorate the summer porch. But new tubers are not a yearly business since gloxinias with good culture last a long time. Fine varieties include Etoile de Feu, a bright red, and King of the Reds, a darker crimson shade. Mont Blanc and Brunhilde are excellent whites. Sky Blue is a light purple; Monterey Rose a soft and lovely deep pink. Emperor Frederick is a white-banded scarlet and Emperor Wilhelm a white-banded, deep violet. My own preference is for the whites, although these are not so easy to propagate, and for Monterey Rose which once gave me six weeks of bloom.

The first gloxinia tubers are potted as early as possible so that at least one flowering potful will grace those first deeply appreciated June hours on the porch. Each tuber is given a four-inch container and covered with an inch of soil. The best mixture feels light and looks dark with coarse leaf mold or rotted compost predominating and a generous mixing in of sand, with two teaspoonfuls of bone meal of any type added, if convenient, for each potful of soil. Only a little garden loam is needed. The aim, as with African violets, is a moisture-retentive, easily penetrated growing mixture. If extra soil for saintpaulias is at hand, use that.

Place the newly potted tubers for the first month in a rather cool place. An east window with heat averaging sixty degrees is ideal. Apply water from the pot saucer and in sparing amounts until growth is well advanced. When several leaves have developed, move the plants to any window where saintpaulias are thriving.

Place gloxinias on the outside porch only after warm weather is well established. These natives of tropical America resent variable spring weather with its chilly nights. It is therefore safer to keep them indoors until June and then to place them outside in light shade and out of strong winds or draughts. When the first buds appear it is worth while, although not absolutely necessary to shift plants to five-inch pots. This extra root room tends to prolong the flowering period and also to increase the size of the tuber for another year.

After two to three weeks or more of flowering, depending on variety, the gloxinia should be tended like other potted plants. Then, unless they seem determined to grow, reduce moisture and let the plants dry out completely. Remove the dead tops and store the tubers in their pots in a dim, dry place until next February. A winter storage temperature of forty-five to fifty degrees is excellent.

In February examine the pots of stored gloxinias. Those which show signs of growth, prepare for a new cycle. Try to hold back the others in storage in order to have successive flowering. Before bringing the pots to a window, scoop out what you can of the top soil. Replace this with a fresh mixture containing plenty of leaf mold or, if you would be extra painstaking, remove the tubers from the pots, shake them free of soil, and repot in a fresh mixture.

Extra feeding is usually unnecessary during the growing period. When soil is only partially renewed you may, if you wish, give an application of liquefied plant tablets or weak liquid cow manure (the dried commercial product is soaked in a pail of water for this purpose) in repeated doses from the pot saucer every three weeks from the time growth is well started until buds form. This extra feeding might be classed as "exhibition tactics" not essential for porch or window plants.

Gloxinia Increase

During the flowering period it is an easy matter to propagate more of any favorite gloxinias except perhaps the whites which sometimes prove temperamental. Simply cut off sharply with its piece of stem any medium-sized leaf and insert this the stem's length in a small pot of moist warm sand. Proceed then as with violets. Some amateurs place an inverted mason jar above the leaf. A miniature greenhouse is thus contrived. In a light not sunny place the leaf will soon begin to develop roots at the stem end. Little extra water will be necessary with the jar over the planting. When a great deal of moisture collects, lift the jar for a few minutes. Not until new leaves begin to push up at the base of the old one is the jar discarded.

Such plants started in August, which seems to be the most propitious time, will set their first flowers in late winter of the next year, since new plants are grown on through their first year and not rested in the manner of mature tubers. The leaf-started plants are transplanted from the first small sand-filled pots to four-inch containers of the regular soil mixture at the time the jar is permanently removed. And in this size they spend many subsequent years.

Gloxinias in mixed colors may be obtained from seed. Sow this before mid-March on the surface of a pot of soil. Firm it in place but do not press soil above it. Cover the pot with a pane of glass and on this lay a piece of paper. Keep the sowing in a seventy-degree place. When after a week—it takes a month for summer sowings—germination takes place, the paper is removed. Turn the piece of glass over as water collects on it. A week or so later remove it often enough to keep it dry but not for such an extended time that the surface soil dries out.

When seedlings are large enough to be handled, they are transplanted to a flat and kept in a light but not sunny place. As size increases they are separately transferred first to two-inch pots and then to four-inch ones. The first year, probably about August, only one flower may appear on a plant. In time there may be fifteen opening at once and perhaps a second flowering almost as fine, if you do not urge your growing plants to hasten to their rest.

Other "Violet" Values

But to return to saintpaulias. Besides being a grand pot plant, it seems the African violet also has value as a cut flower. Try sometime for a unique centerpiece, an arrangement, in a flat dish, of concentric circles of blossoms placed according to color sequence. If the dish or plate you are using is dark, commence with a few deep-toned violets in the center and let your scheme pass through the dark and paler blues to lavender and pink. Then place a whole final circle of white in direct contrast to the blue or green china.

If you are using a white saucer, glass plate, or Dresden soup bowl perhaps, place white flowers for the center motif and let the final ring be blue. A sprig of rosy apple blossoms with a few green leaves, a bit of lavender lilac, a rosebud or fully opened blossom also makes a pleasing center accent. And incidentally you don't need to cut flowers for these flat arrangements. Those lovely blossoms which plants constantly discard may be gathered up for the purpose. They have plenty of life and beauty remaining, once they reach a refreshing bowl of water.

Corsages

Corsages of saintpaulias are also a practical and beautiful possibility. Regina Zacharias, an enthusiast in Wichita, Kansas, has made lovely bouquets of purple and pink saintpaulias alone or in combination with roses. She has successfully used several varieties and tells me the flowers keep fresh a whole evening. It is essential to select fairly long-stemmed sprays and to cut them far enough ahead to steep them for several hours in a glass of water. Let the water come right up to the flower heads so that the stems will absorb a good supply of moisture for this special performance. Mrs. Zacharias, who just happened to make a saintpaulia corsage when a fifteen-year-old friend was attending her first formal, also suggests topping presents with a little bunch of "violets." In winter particularly they make such a sprightly and appealing addition to attractive gift wrappings.

I must add that Mrs. Zacharias certainly belongs to the saintpaulia fraternity, or is it a sorority? She reports eighty blooms on one plant at one time and when first she wrote me late one January, she counted forty-six on a white variety grown without sunshine in a north window. Her plants are arranged before a wall of glass brick built just for their display. These plants are *kept standing* in a little water and when transplanting is done, twice a year, pots are broken apart to avoid any possible leaf injury in the transfer. A small amount of the old soil is broken off each time and some fresh added. This is composed of half and half garden soil and old manure.

Mrs. Zacharias gives many plants away and is sometimes pained to hear that the new owner has not been successful. I am sure we all sympathize with her gentle commentary, "I do think that no one should grow saintpaulias who is not a true lover of flowers."

CHAPTER SEVEN

Greenhouse Program

OPENING the door of a little greenhouse filled with saintpaulias is like lifting the lid of a box of precious stones, so jewel-like are the pure tones of amethyst purple, translucent rose, and iridescent pearly white. Even a small eight-by-ten glasshouse will accommodate a large and representative collection and still leave space enough for propagating and hybridizing. A small, well-run setup might even maintain itself profitably with just a limited amount of selling.

The man or woman who is interested in an absorbing and profitable business in saintpaulias will be wise seriously to consider building a greenhouse for their more extensive growing under controlled conditions of light, heat, and ventilation. Several thriving concerns I know have been developed by amateurs who in the beginning grew African violets at a window just for their own pleasure. Only gradually and almost unintentionally did they turn from being hobbyists to being growers. They saw opportunity all around them, however, especially in the increasing demand for rarer varieties like the doubles, and crinkled- and ruffled-leaved types, the various bicolors, and the plants with flowers of unusual shadings.

The large commercial houses, catering to the demands of florists, do not often find this specialist trade worth while, but for the "little fellow" in business the hobbyist and collector are good customers.

If you are inexperienced in running a greenhouse, the following brief generalities on management will help you through the first experimental year of your fascinating venture. After that time, you will have arrived at an almost automatic schedule with heating, ventilating, and watering no longer matters of crisis or special concern. Very likely you will be heating by hot water which is generally preferred for a small greenhouse.

Heating

It may be that you can proceed economically and heat the glasshouse attached to your dwelling from the same boiler that heats your house, if this boiler is for either steam or hot water. If it is a steam boiler, by placing a check valve in the return line, a false water line can be established in the heating coils that go through the greenhouse. Hot water from the steam boiler circulates through the heating coils and does not interfere with the house heating system. An automatic device is used to circulate the water. Oil heaters for the small greenhouse are also available at low cost. The warm air is circulated from the heater by a small electric fan which sends it down to the floor where the heat is needed. Both of these heating systems can be thermostatically controlled.

At first, it will help you in your routine decisions if you realize that the aim is to run a greenhouse so that it will approximate the conditions of a natural day for saint-paulias. All changes of atmosphere should be gradual with about a ten-degree drop in temperature at night—just as it occurs in nature when the sun goes down. Through the day a seventy- to seventy-five-degree temperature is suitable, though daytime heat, provided there is ventilation, may run as high as eighty-five degrees without harming saintpaulias. At night, sixty-five degrees is low enough. Below that, growth and bloom are noticeably checked.

Shading

With African violets, shading of the house is usually necessary throughout the year, although in the Pacific Northwest one large commercial grower finds it better to keep the glass clear in November, December, and January. You will probably find it best to dim the light by maintaining a coat of whitewash on the glass, or to cover it for more permanent effect with a thin coat of white or green paint. Cloth hung inside is, of course, the best way to provide shade since it also protects plants during ventilation from the drip of rain or snow and so avoids spotting of foliage. Roller slat shades are another possibility. Shading with these can be a much more exact business and they are far less trouble than the old-fashioned whitewash coatings.

Watering

Plan to water your plants in the morning as the temperature of the day rises. Plants should not go into the night wet. In winter once a day always suffices and sometimes but once or twice a week. Ten a.m. is a good time. In spring and fall, watering is usually on alternate days. In summer saintpaulias will need more. Take a look at them about 10 a.m. and again at 2 p.m. Very likely you will find them thirsty both times and you will not want to risk dryness to the point where the foliage wilts. Whenever the weather is dark and evaporation is slow, as is likely through December and January, take care to moisten only the soil and not the foliage. Overwatering during sunless stretches may start an attack of leaf splotch.

The best method is to go over the plants, pot by pot, watering them safely at the rim from a slow-running nozzle or, if the number is not too extensive, you can use a dipper. It is so important that the water be unchilled. Take care that it keeps to room temperature or a little above. As the season wanes and the hose water gets very cold, temper it with enough hot water from the boiler to take off the chill, or if your greenhouse is small, keep a large tub of water under a bench. This will hold a large enough supply to dip out for your needs and it will always be of agreeable room temperature.

Pest and Disease Control

A clean and tidy greenhouse is the best possible check to insect and disease. Pick off discolored leaves and gather up the constantly discarded flowers of saintpaulias. Where bits of foliage or other vegetation collect and decay on benches or walks, disease finds an inspiring breeding ground. It is all I can do when I walk through a greenhouse and see these danger spots not to ask for a paper bag and impolitely start a gathering and burning project all on my own.

A thorough yearly housecleaning with everything moved out of the house is also essential. While the plants are outside give the house a fumigation with cyanimide, G Grade, following carefully the directions given. Cynogas, to be used when the house is emptied of plants, is a very strong material. It is fatal to any human who breathes it. It is not for the dwelling or lean-to glasshouse and while a greenhouse is being fumigated, it should be locked up and "posted" with warning signs. With these precautions Cynogas can be confidently used, as it has been successfully by many gardeners for many years.

When fumigating, follow directions carefully. With Fumetobac, for instance, allow a four and one-half-inch pot of the material for every five thousand cubic feet of greenhouse space. Spread this out on the fumigating tins, light it, and then get out quickly. To compute number of cubic feet use this formula:

$a = \text{length} \times \text{width}$

$b = \text{height at ridge} + \text{height at eaves} \div 2$

$a \times b = \text{cubic feet of house}$

Some growers also consider it good mite-deterrence to maintain a layer of naphthalene flakes or camphor balls on the benches to an extent where the odor is noticeable as one enters from outside. Others consider this treatment hardly worth while.

Decide upon a regular spray program to coincide with your convenience and the health of the saintpaulias. Hit-or-miss spraying when you at last find time is wasteful in every way since it fails to deter, and deterring pest and disease is far easier than controlling them. In fact, control in some cases is just about impossible. When mealy bug or mite reach the stage of serious infestation, your procedure is all too likely to be—discard.

It is a good plan to spray the greenhouse once a week. Choose a cloudy morning and carefully use one of the all-purpose preparations according to the manufacturer's directions. Wilson's O.K. plant spray, Seagreen, and Hitox, as well as a number of others, are good. It is better to alternate materials than to depend entirely on one. An all-purpose spray regularly applied—plus one monthly substitution of fumigation with a nicotine material like Fumetobac or Nicofume—should keep saintpaulias free of mealy bug, aphis, and mite.

The favorite spray of one large commercial house is Turkey Red—15 ounces Sulphanated Castor Oil; 25 ounces Rotonone, 4 or 5 per cent; 27 ounces Alcoholic Pyrethrum; mixed in 50 gallons of warm water. DDT is also being tried out in various strengths. Used at a fifteen per cent strength it does not harm plants, but also it does not sufficiently harm pests so that stronger treatments are being attempted. According to one of the largest and most successful wholesale men with whom I have discussed this, to date DDT is not considered worth using on saintpaulias.

African violets are indeed plants of tender foliage. Their succulent leaves and delicate blooms are easily damaged by many of the sprays, although the plants themselves seem to have an inherent power to recover from spray injury. Still the cure seems to be worse than the curse if a whole house of plants must be spotted and the flowers browned to insure health for, of course, under such conditions, commercial value is temporarily gone.

Sodium Selenate

Commercial growers are doing interesting work with Sodium Selenate which has a holdover value of approximately three months. Ohio State University reports that "Selenium is fairly safe on African violets, provided they are well established in the pot in which they are growing." For those whose plants are in a greenhouse where treatment is indicated on a larger scale, this advice is given in the *Monthly Bulletin* (March, 1947) of the Ohio Florists' Association:

SODIUM SELENATE. This material which is absorbed by the plant through the roots, kills red spider, mites . . . and does a fair job on aphids. It will not kill root nematodes. Available as P-40 or as a powder; applications every three months are necessary as it leaches readily from the soil.

P-40 is applied at 3 pounds per 100 square feet. The pure sodium selenate is made into a stock solution by dissolving 1 pound in 4½ gallons of water. Use the stock solution in the following ways:

1. Spray tank
    1 quart in 25 gallons water—treats 100 square feet
    2 quarts in 50 gallons water—treats 200 square feet

1 gallon in 100 gallons water—treats 400 square feet

2. Hozon nozzle (Four Power Co., Warrensville, O.)
1 quart placed in a pail and 7 quarts water added.
When the 8 quarts (2 gallons) of solution in the
pail have been siphoned, only 100 square feet of
bench area should be covered.

The above methods apply sodium selenate at ¼ gram
per square foot. Before selenium is applied, make sure
the plants are well established in the pots or bench,
otherwise it may be fatal. *Soil should be moist* and an
even job of distribution is essential. For pot plants,
apply the same as you would a liquid fertilizer. Selenium appears to be safe on many cut flower and pot
plant crops.

Ventilating

Proper ventilation of a greenhouse, large or small is
most important. Although saintpaulias like it warm, they
do not thrive in a close "dead" air. Even through the winter a fresh "buoyant" atmosphere must be maintained.
Only during periods of extreme cold and storm should you
leave ventilators closed for a twenty-four hour stretch.

Spring and fall are critical times when there may be
considerable dampness in the greenhouse. During these
seasons it is advisable to leave the ventilators open a bit
to maintain the proper humidity, even when the heat is
on. Ventilators also help to maintain the required temperature. Although the day temperature is kept as near
seventy degrees as possible, on summer days the heat will

soar dangerously above this, if the ventilators are not open to admit cooler air. In cold weather, fresh air is usually admitted from the roof so there will not be a draft on the plants. Frequently a netting of cheesecloth is hung underneath the ventilators to prevent draft.

Ventilation is also helpful in maintaining humidity when the greenhouse becomes dry due to the artificial heat of the heating system. Sprinkling the walks with water and admitting fresh air from outside helps to maintain the humidity required. Automatic electric ventilation, thermostatically controlled, is now available for small greenhouses. By this means the ventilators open when the sun hits the greenhouse and heats it above the required temperature. They close when the sun goes under clouds or goes down at the end of the day.

Without automatic control, ventilation requires fairly regular attention along with that judgment which comes with experience. Through the summer and early in fall keep the ventilators open all the time, day and night, unless the weather is unseasonably cool or storm threatens. Then, of course, ventilators must be closed to avoid the damage of a ripping wind. As night temperatures drop toward the thirties, close the ventilators tightly at sundown. Then open them in the morning as sunshine warms the house.

Greenhouse Calendar

Here are a few month-by-month suggestions for running a greenhouse.

SEPTEMBER. Actually this is the beginning of the

greenhouse year, not January, for it is now that the days grow cool, and heat, the most important aspect of greenhouse procedure, must be turned on. Heat automatically if you can with oil, coal, or a stoker thermostatically controlled. Then the temperature will stay right where you set it.

In any case inspect the heating system now to see that it is in fine working condition well before you need it.

Sometimes September is surprising. A sudden cold spell is no time to get in the repair man or to send away for replacement of equipment. The forehanded, of course, tend to the heating system in June. In case you didn't, clean the smoke pipe right away, oil the hinges, check the insulation on the boiler, change the water, and vent air from the heating coils. If there are pumps and motors in connection with the system, oil them or have them checked by an electrician to make sure they are in good operating order.

When night temperatures can no longer be definitely maintained at sixty-five degrees, or nights keep persistently damp and cool so that the greenhouse has a "creepy" atmosphere early each morning, turn on the heat. Do this even if you seem to be wasting fuel by keeping the ventilators open through most of the day. Cold and dampness are not the saintpaulias' friends and you must take care now that plants do not get off to a poor start for the winter.

The exact date for turning on the heat even in a given locality varies considerably and often as much as two to three weeks from one year to another.

Even without heat keep ventilators open through most of the day. Never be hidebound by schedule. Judge the conditions as they are, not as the calendar indicates they should be.

Fill up the soil bins with your favorite mixture well before frost. You will be doing plenty of potting-up and shifting-on before spring.

Spray one day a week for three weeks. The fourth week fumigate. Maintain this schedule throughout the year.

Water daily and with care. And always temper the hose water, which even in summer runs harmfully cool for saintpaulias, with enough hot water from the boiler to take the chill off and keep the water near the prevailing temperature of the greenhouse. This precaution, you recall, is the best possible preventative to leaf spot. If your greenhouse is quite small, keep a large tub of water under a bench. This will hold enough water for all your plants and you can be certain then that it is room temperature.

OCTOBER. Gradually decrease the amount of water given to plants as days grow shorter and the daytime heat of the house stays closer to a seventy-degree average. Watering by the end of the month, or sooner, should be on an alternate-day schedule.

Close the ventilators at night. Open them, more or less fully, as weather indicates, about ten o'clock each morning.

Start little-and-often feedings of extra nourishment (unless you are of the no-fertilizer school). Every three or four weeks water with weak liquid manure—a covered

crock of it under a greenhouse bench is a wonderful asset
—Chem Salts, (1 tablespoonful to 1 gallon water), Hypo-
nex or some favorite brand of your own. This procedure
usually means larger flowers of finer color and handsomer
leaves too.

Stop extra feedings if weeks of prolonged dull weather
begin to slow up plant growth. Be watchful of ventilation during these "heavy" days.

Shift plants as they need it. Unless you are cramped
for space or trying to make every inch of bench space
count commercially, move plants on to roomier quarters
often enough for them to develop into fine spreading specimens not high-bunched pot plants. (With special feeding, as Mrs. Wright practises it, spreading plants are also
possible in small pots which restrict root systems.)

As last spring's leaves develop new plant colonies, pot
these up separately in number threes.

NOVEMBER. Continue the winter-maintenance program now established.

Spray weekly and fumigate monthly. Be vigilant. If
any insect attack gets ahead of you, spray every third day
until it is cleaned up. Beware of accepting into your greenhouse any plants in either healthy or ailing condition.
Protect your fine collection. Segregate newcomers until
you are *sure* they carry no mite. Steel yourself to discard
any badly infested plants of your own.

Dull days are here now and for perhaps eight weeks
to come, so avoid overwatering. Twice a week may now
suffice.

Ventilate judiciously so as not to chill.

Sow seed at any time ripe pods of it are available.

DECEMBER. Remove from the sides of plants any noticeably overlarge leaves. Don't mind nipping a few out of the center too. This is a particularly good thing to do six weeks before you wish "to crop" flowers. An open crown and not too much leaf growth promotes flowering.

If stems of larger leaves become jellylike, consider whether the house is being kept too damp and too cool. Try propping up the outer leaves of large and shapely plants with pipe-cleaner supports. Those damp, cool pot rims on which leaves rest, promote this undesirable condition.

Send as Christmas presents to your saintpaulia friends, leaves from some of your choicest varieties (though, of course, not of patented kinds). Let the outside wrappings be festive, but inside observe the practicalities of packing with the leaf dry and the stem moist. Label "Open at once; don't wait till Christmas!"

JANUARY, FEBRUARY, MARCH. As days lengthen, African violets burgeon. Feed with a freer hand now, if you notice that growth is developing and more and more buds are in evidence with the advancing year.

Shade more, if it is necessary, on bright winter mornings.

Take leaf cuttings in abundance. They seem to root more quickly now than at any other season. Leaves taken at this time should mean fine three-inch pot plants for autumn selling, when everyone gets interested in house plants again.

In dull, muggy weather, be particularly mindful of

greenhouse cleanliness. Pick off imperfect or unhealthy leaves. Gather the faded flowers so freely dropped each day. A clean greenhouse means healthy stock.

APRIL and MAY. Ventilate more freely. Shade more carefully. Water more abundantly.

Take as many leaf cuttings as space and time permit. Do a little hybridizing, being careful to keep accurate records so you'll know what you have when at last you get it!

Try your hand at corsage-making.

Spare a few sprays of saintpaulias to arrange in a little vase for your desk with true violet leaves and a few yellow primroses and stars of Bethlehem from the outdoor garden.

JUNE. Turn off the heat, weather permitting, which it usually does.

Keep the ventilators open during the day, but only "cracked" at night.

Water daily, as necessary, but still observe the precautions of keeping the water warm.

Select a few specimen plants for the veranda. Arrange them on a white wire stand out of wind and sun. Place ferns and vines among them.

JULY. Take a vacation from your own "violets" but don't hesitate to journey in a direction where other saintpaulias grow. Hobbyists enjoy meeting other hobbyists, to compare notes on culture, convictions on varieties.

But leave in charge of your greenhouse someone of at least average saintpaulia intelligence. And with him leave a *written* list of directions.

AUGUST. This is clean-up month and a big job. At some time, if you can, remove to the porch all your plants and give the house a thorough cleaning. If that's impossible, clear out and clean up by sections.

Remove the layers of ashes or other material with which benches have been covered. Remove the sand from the propagating bench. Empty any tubs or pools. Wash down benches and floors. Wash windows so that not a trace of green scum is visible. But don't slosh too much water about because your plants have to come back by nightfall. Apply by hand a light "snowfall" of agricultural lime. This will deter fungous growth. Cover the benches again with a one-half- to three-quarter-inch layer of sifted coal ashes, washed stone chips, clean sand, or best of all, round, graded gravel.

Now or at any other convenient time when the cutting bench can be emptied, prepare it with fresh sand. Sterilize this with a drenching of boiling water. Then cover with heavy paper or a piece of clean carpet to hold the heat until everything undesirable is destroyed.

Take care of the heating system. It is your most vital piece of equipment. It is wiser to clean and grease now than to wait until September when use is again imminent.

And don't keep so busy you forget to have fun. Growing saintpaulias, lots of them, is a grand business. Enjoy it!

Quarantine Regulations

If you are going in for saintpaulias commercially and live in a horticultural zone quarantined because of Japanese beetle infestation, your shipments will have to be made under government procedure and inspection. Write to your county agricultural agent for particulars. If you do not know who he is, write to the Department of Agriculture in the capital city of your state for information. Then you can make arrangements to have a representative of the department regularly fumigate the house in which saintpaulias are grown for shipping. He will also sterilize the potting soil to be used for plants so that it will be free of any grubs. Then periodically he will inspect to be sure regulations are being regarded and give you, if requirements are met, a certificate to permit shipping.

Saintpaulia leaves, which carry no earth, may be sent free of inspection. Plants destined for intershipping zones in already infested "beetle areas" need not be inspected. (In addition to Japanese beetle trouble some of the southern states are infested with the white-fringed beetle. All persons living in infested areas must also comply with the quarantine regulations pertaining to this insect.)

If all this seems unduly irksome to you, it is only because you have never seen the Japanese beetle working untrammeled and at the height of his powers. I once lived near Riverton, New Jersey, where the beetles were first introduced to this country. It was nothing to see them turn a velvet golf green into a piece of old hay in a week. Trees were defoliated. Roses ruined.

Beetle control is necessary so do your part and be patient with the inspector who has to do his!

CHAPTER EIGHT

Pest and Disease

IT IS QUITE possible to grow African violets successfully over a period of years and only rarely have to deal with pest or disease. Especially if plants are all home-reared and kept culturally content is there little danger of ailments. Like a happy child, a happy plant is usually a healthy one. One collector who has some two hundred plants reports but two specimens attacked by mealy bug in seven years, about three with crown rot, and only two with mite—none now that she practices isolation of unknowns.

If you receive plants from outside sources—greenhouse or home—it is really most important to grow them apart from your other plants for about two months. It rarely takes this long to diagnose mite, yet if a newly purchased plant had recently been infested, the trouble could go unnoticed for this length of time before newly formed leaves unfurled to confirm your suspicions. After two months you can be sure of their condition and safely let them mingle with your own healthy stock. In tending violets during the trial period, wash your hands before you go near other plants, even to water them.

I do not mean to infer that florist's stock is likely to be

unhealthy or infested. It is just that an occasional plant, which he has every reason to believe to be in first-rate condition, will sometimes, particularly under less ideal home conditions, become a prey to a disease or pest which greenhouse conditions kept in abeyance.

There are seven possible troubles—two diseases and five pests.

Ring Spot

Ring spot we have mentioned. It is characterized by yellow rings on the upper surfaces of a dark green leaf. It is caused by too much direct sunlight, or by the application to soil or foliage of water of a temperature varying more than five degrees from that of the temperature of the room in which the plants are growing. Ring spot is easy to avoid. Moisten or spray only with room-temperature water.

Crown and Leaf-Stem Rot

Crown rot may occur when plants are divided—a process to handle most delicately. If after the separation and repotting of a plant, the leaves get limp and lose their good color, and the plant rapidly declines, it is usually because this fungous organism has found entry at some point of bruised or cut tissue. To deter rot, it is wise, when plants are newly divided, to keep them on the dry side until wounded areas heal over and a new root system begins to form.

Sometimes crown rot is started by overwatering. The fungus which produces the ailment is present in most fertile soils so that any unhealthy condition may make it flare up. Mr. Holley, working at the University of New Hampshire, observed that plants under home conditions were often affected in the late spring when furnace heat is first shut off. "At this time the air becomes considerably more moist and the plant requires a great deal less water. Yet water is often applied at the same rate as in winter. Then some plants begin wilting and eventually rot off. Control of this trouble is primarily a matter of watering."

There is another condition of rot which affects the stems of the leaves, especially of the older leaves which droop over and touch the sides of the pot. These leaf stems or petioles may become jellylike, while the leaves deteriorate and eventually die. Mr. Holley's explanation is this. Since "the African violet has no way of shedding its leaves like other plants, this quite often is only a method of shedding the older leaves. If these are regularly removed when they get out-size, the rotting often ceases. This condition might be aggravated, however, by any conditions which make other plants drop leaves. A common cause could be lack of plant food. In every case where a plant begins yellowing its leaves because of an exhausted soil, it also drops some of them over the edge of the pot and these become soft and die. Regular shifting and feeding and good culture will keep this trouble at a minimum."

It is also good practice to keep leaf stems from resting on the pot rim. A pipe-stem cleaner is a handy gadget to insert in the pot at the soil's edge. The end of the cleaner can be loosely looped around petiole so as to hold it a little higher than it would naturally grow.

Aphids or Plant Lice

Aphids or plant lice sometimes cluster on the new young growth of plants. Usually an occasional washing of leaves controls them, and mealy bugs too. If detected before an infestation is advanced, several successive daily sprayings with lukewarm water will destroy them. It is even possible to free a plant of aphids by holding it on its side under a slow-running faucet and carefully turning it so that the stream of water cleanses all the affected growth.

When aphids have become established, two treatments are possible—a soapy spray or dip with a nicotine preparation like Black Leaf 40 added, or a spray with an oil material like Volck. If nicotine is used, prepare a solution of room-temperature suds by adding soap flakes to hot water, getting it foamy, and then letting it stand for an hour in the room where the "violet" is growing. Add the liquid nicotine then, according to directions, and spray thoroughly. Or immerse the plant completely for ten minutes in a deep vessel of the soapy solution. Then remove it, spray gently with clear warm water to remove any adhering soil particles, and let the foliage dry off in the shade—to avoid crown rot and leaf spot—before returning the plant to the window. In stubborn cases it may be necessary to repeat this treatment once or twice at weekly intervals.

If you prefer to attack aphids with Volck, prepare a spray or dip of one teaspoonful to one quart of warm water. Use the cleansing water spray afterward and dry off the plant as suggested in the nicotine treatment. Repeat at weekly intervals, if necessary. A third treatment with Sodium Selenate has limited possibilities. (See below under Cyclamen Mite.)

Mealy Bug

Ailing plants inevitably invite the mealy bug, that cottony pest which clusters in colonies deep in the crowns of plants and hides on the underside of leaves. Mealy bugs exhaust and destroy plants by extracting cell sap through their sucking mouth parts. Piercing each bug with a needle, pen point, or toothpick will, if patience survives the process, get a plant clean in the course of weeks or even months.

This pricking of larger bugs, especially at the beginning of an attack is really not too tedious. The main thing is to get them before they attain the mature or egg-laying stage. Sometimes an alcohol-dipped swab, or small paintbrush, can be used to advantage, but the delicate brittle nature of stems and leaves makes this treatment, or the one involving lemon oil, fairly dangerous because these materials may burn the delicate foliage.

Change the swab as necessary in treating a badly infested plant but keep at the job until every white cluster vanishes. When the plant finally appears clean, hold it on its side under the faucet and let a gentle stream of warm water wash off the alcohol, which has a very drying effect on plant tissues.

It is really wise to discard a badly infested plant before others are affected. However, if many valued speci-

mens are involved it may seem worth while to prepare a
dip or spray of Volck, a miscible oil preparation. (One
of those small sprayers which come with moth-proofing
outfits can be used.) Follow the manufacturer's directions exactly and treat the plant top at two- to three-week
intervals until it is clean again. *But it is better to avoid
than to try to cure the mealy bug.* Occasional fine water
syringing of foliage on bright days is a good control.
Keep plants out of the sun then until leaves are dry.

It may be, however, that DDT will eventually solve
this insect problem as it has others. One correspondent,
whose husband is a research chemist, after failing to free
her plants of mealy bug by the usual treatments, successfully tried the new chemical. She reports:

"Several months ago each plant was treated with
DDT. The preparation was 50 per cent DDT powder,
50 per cent talc powder. Application was made by a
camel's-hair brush, touching the bugs where seen and
then dusting the crown and bases of leaf and flower
stems with the powder. The bugs fell off, apparently
dead, within the hour. Daily inspections showed no
more bugs at any time for the following two weeks, nor
has there been a sign of them since. The one application
required to cure the trouble consumed very little powder, probably about two grains per plant, and the part
of it which dropped to the earth around the crown of
plant has done no harm."

Seed houses now carry a ten per cent strength of
DDT for this purpose. One ounce will provide an ample supply for anyone raising African violets on the

household scale of house plants. But growers, it must be said, have not had this correspondent's success.

Cyclamen Mite

The cyclamen mite also attacks the African violet. This is a pest you will know by its effect rather than by its appearance, since it is visible only with the aid of a hand lens. Furthermore, it works inside terminal buds and so is out of the reach of sprays. Plants which have been attacked by mites show the result of infestation even in the early stages. Growth in general is dwarfed, and leaves, particularly in the center of the plant, are deformed and reduced in size. Hairiness is more pronounced than on healthy plants and leaves tend to be cupped upward or rolled downward. If plants are not so sickly that blooming is entirely suppressed, they will produce only malformed blossoms, or set buds which fail to open.

If you detect these symptoms on a plant, segregate it immediately and after tending it, be sure to wash your hands before touching other plants. Mites spread by contact so you cannot be too careful, particularly if you have a large collection.

Infestations have also been cleaned up by placing a plant overnight in a large, tightly fastened grocery bag with a liberal scattering of naphthalene flakes in the bottom. With this treatment care must be taken to keep the flakes from touching the foliage and to treat plants only when the soil is fairly dry. The fumigating treatment may have to be repeated in the course of several months until all possible cycles of the mites have developed.

From Mrs. Odom comes this report of her naphthalene-flake treatment: "I fashion a miniature fumigation room from a large kettle with a lid, a water bath canner, empty, of course. I use from fifteen to twenty moth balls, taking care to treat plants only when the soil is quite dry. Excess moisture in the soil seems to form a gas which burns the leaves and will even kill the plant. . . . I leave each plant or group of plants in my 'fumigator' for twelve hours—all day or all night."

In greenhouses, the flakes are thickly scattered on the benches and more added when the camphor odor is no longer noticeable to one entering from the outdoors.

There are two courses open to the owner of an infested plant—discard it, or give it the hot water treatment.

The hot water immersion treatment, from my own observation, is both safe and sure. There are those, however, both specialists and amateurs, who have found that the cure kills or else so adversely affects growth that, though mites are destroyed, plants never regain health. Mr. Holley considers the treatment lethal, as does the College of Agriculture at the Ohio State University which reports, "We don't believe in the hot water treatment for mite because most of the time when the plants are dipped . . . the mite is killed, and so is the plant. If the plant isn't killed, it is so weakened that you have to throw it away anyway."

But Mrs. Freed has found that if foliage is carefully

handled so that it is not bruised or broken in the course
of treatment, plants are not otherwise damaged. She
either isolates or uses the hot water immersion as pre-
cautionary treatment for every plant added to her collection. It depends on whether she has the time for immersing or the room for isolation!

The hot water treatment is the contribution of P. P.
Pirone of the New Jersey Agricultural Experiment Station to African violet culture. He writes:

You will find it relatively easy to clean up the infestation in short order by immersing the plant, pot
and all, for 15 minutes in water kept at 110 degrees.
At this temperature and exposure all stages of mites
will be destroyed without any appreciable harm to the
plant.

Naturally you will want to use a fairly accurate
thermometer for the job. Unless the water is hot
enough, you'll be wasting your time, and if the water
is too hot, say 120 degrees, you'll soon be in the
market for another plant!

The container for the treatment should be large
and deep enough so that the water in it will cover
the plant completely. Heat the water to 110 degrees
and have another pan of even hotter water ready. Set
the plant in the first container and add enough of the
hotter water to bring the temperature back quickly to
110 degrees. Stir the water around the plant constantly with a wooden spoon during the 15-minute
treatment. Watch the thermometer closely, and add

more hot water when needed to keep the temperature as near 110 degrees as possible.

After 15 minutes lift the plant out and tilt the pot to drain off the excess water. Then set the pot upright and shade the plant for a day or two with newspaper. Afterwards, the plant can be set back in its favored spot in the house. Incidentally, if soil particles get on the foliage during the dipping, they can be rinsed off either immediately after the treatment or after the shade has been removed.

This treatment may sound complicated but it really isn't difficult to carry out. It is the surest way I know of completely eradicating mites from African violets. Moreover, the plant will be entirely free of mites in the future, provided, of course, that reinfestation does not occur from other plants in the vicinity harboring mites.

Several experiment stations are also working with a Sodium Selenate soil treatment to render plants *immune* to aphids and mites (but not mealy bug, unfortunately) for a year or even much longer. The extent of control is still not known, although experimental work at the Ohio State University indicates a lasting benefit for five or six months. Claim has been made of some residual effect over a period of years. This would be a grand thing. Because of the extremely poisonous nature of this material, however, in your home you are not yet advised to use it on plants. The aim is eventually to make up the material in tablet form and sell "with fool-proof directions."

Springtails

A pest which at this point remains unclassified is one which we temporarily describe as springtail. A narrow white object, it appears in soil and swarms out of the drainage hole at the bottom at times of watering. Evidentally springtails do not get on leaves or blossoms or apparently interfere with blooming. Just what they do do is not certain and the main complaint against them comes from growers whose customers notice the tiny insect and are wary of buying plants so infested. Watering the soil with Black Leaf 40 helps. Stronger solutions which have rid plants of the pest have caused such severe injury to growth as to be of questionable value. Doubtless the future holds the solution of the springtail problem which the present does not reveal.

Thrips

Finally there is thrip, an insect which is all too familiar to outdoor gardeners who grow the gladiolus. On African violets this almost invisible pest reveals its presence by white streaks on the flower petals. These are particularly apparent on the dark-flowering varieties, and are made by the rasping habit of the insect. Another indication of thrip is the premature falling of flowers. Usually blooms last through a week or more. When plants harbor thrips, blooms drop in one or two days because the insects pollinate the flowers. Naturally this causes the setting of seed and the swift fall of flowers, which is the preamble. In some cases several weekly dustings with DDT have cleaned up an infestation.

CHAPTER NINE

Clubs, Societies, and Shows

IN RECENT years the saintpaulia has achieved horticultural dignity. Like the rose, the gladiolus, and the delphinium it reached in 1946 the organized status of national recognition. The African Violet Society of America was formed in Atlanta, Georgia, to study normalities and vagaries and to unravel the decidedly duplicatory nomenclature. Plans were made for a national show in 1947.

Heretofore the African violet had simply been an appealing house plant not quite so popular perhaps as the geranium and begonia. Today it is at the top with professional greenhouse men and amateur window gardeners alike fascinated by its hybridization and culture. Indeed, it has become business on a big scale but with growers still unable to supply the tremendous demand for the newer varieties.

Until 1946 there was no printed information on the plant aside from articles in magazines, except in a small pamphlet which I wrote for the *Ladies' Home Journal*. Requests for this pamphlet passed the 50,000 mark in a few months to the complete bewilderment of a staff used to milder horticultural demands. Meanwhile, Round

Robin groups, sponsored by the magazine, *Flower Grower* served as a means of contact for enthusiasts. Members had a wonderful time exchanging leaves to extend their collections and exchanging much useful information, too, on how to grow bigger, better, and healthier saint-paulias.

Round Robins

This is the way the thirty-seven Round Robins devoted to the culture of the African violet reach over three hundred and fifty devotees. Applicants send their requests for membership in an Elementary or an Advanced Robin to the director, Miss Marion P. Thomas, in care of *Flower Grower*, 2049 Grand Central Terminal, New York 17, New York. No fee is necessary. The only requirements are that you mail on to the next member, after a stated interval, the group of letters which constitute your Robin and that you send a postcard to the director of your Robin to inform her you have done so. You may or may not, as you wish, include a letter of your own introducing yourself to the group and relaying some of your own observations on saintpaulias.

It is amazing what friendships have been developed via Round Robins. Eventually many members visit each other, even though they live far apart. Ardent collectors enjoy the personal meetings and the opportunity to see each other's plants. Indeed, to many of us, there seems no better reason for taking a trip than to visit a "violet" friend and her plants. This winter even a blizzard which seriously affected transportation did not prevent the planned meeting at Mrs. Freed's in Pennsylvania of Miss Wilcox from western Pennsylvania, Mr. and Mrs. Orrell from Maryland, and Mrs. Newnham, Miss Hagerty, and me from Philadelphia. In fact, those handsome plants of Mrs. Freed's rewarded us for the hardships and hazards of the trip and looked all the lovelier for the drifts of snow seen through the windows.

In case you have always supposed that Round Robins had something to do with the flight of birds, I must tell you that that is modern usage only. Round Robin is a corruption of the French for "round ribbon." When French soldiers wished to petition their superiors and no one wanted to be the first to sign the petition, they used an endless ribbon of paper so that no one wrote first. This in time developed in England into letters passed within a circle of friends.

The African Violet Magazine, a quarterly published by the African Violet Society of America at 2694 Lenox Road N. E., Atlanta, Georgia, also includes a department for the exchange of information. Under the heading, Homing Pigeon, subscribers agree, disagree, argue, and exclaim in print as only ardent horticulturists can. The conductress of this interesting department is Mrs. Freed.

The First Show

Despite these minor signs of popularity, no one had any conception of the breadth of national interest in saintpaulias until the H. G. Hastings Company in Atlanta sponsored in the autumn of 1946, an exhibit in their showroom. Mr. Charles J. Hudson, Jr., of that company was as surprised as everybody else at the success of the project which he directed. He reported:

The traffic jam in front of the Hastings store rated newspaper headlines, and reports in the press told how extra policemen had to be assigned to keep the crowd orderly before the show opened. In a word, African violets took Atlanta by storm!

Considering publicity and promotion, it was by far the greatest, in point of interest and attendance, of any similar show ever staged in the South. There was also the greatest interest in club promotion ever seen in the Atlanta area, there being two African violet societies formed on the evening of November 8.

To get down to statistics, 203 persons exhibited 478 individual plants in the show. About 1,500 people were expected to view the exhibition. . . . A very conservative estimate, however, was that 8,000 people attended over the two days. Visitors came from 103 cities and towns in 14 states—Georgia, South Carolina, North Carolina, Virginia, Alabama, Tennessee, Florida, Michigan, Iowa, Maryland, Pennsylvania, Ohio, Indiana and Texas. Exhibits came from five states—Georgia, Tennessee, Alabama, South Carolina and North Carolina.

Among the many letters—from 29 states—asking for particulars about the show, there were a number inquiring if the rumored yellow African violet would be on display. Apparently hundreds of growers had heard of this elusive color but no one had ever seen it. As a matter of fact, however, there is no such color as yellow in the genus saintpaulia. The varieties exhibited at the show, 32 of them, included Blue Boy, Blue Boy Improved, Commander, Mentor Boy, Neptune, Sailor Boy, Blue Bird, Blue Girl, Topaz Sapphire, Blue and White, Ionantha, Ionantha Grandiflora, Norseman, Amethyst, Lavender Lady, Blue Eyes, Pink Beauty, DuPont Pink, White Lady, Orchid Beauty, Trilby, Plum Pink, Mary Wac, Orchid Lady, Bicolor, Red Bicolor, Red Head, DuPont Blue, Dwarf Orchid, S-22 Bicolor, Blushing Lady, Pink Lady, Blush Beauty and a variety listed as Variegated Leaf Sport.

The new African Violet Society of America, Incorporated, elected as its first president Mrs. O. E. Kellar of Des Moines, Iowa. She has been working with saintpaulias for twenty years and has helped many a neophyte to success with her wonderfully informative personal letters. As Ferne Kellar she is an unmet friend to scores of enthusiasts. The first vice-president chosen was Charles J. Hudson, Jr. of Decatur, Georgia, who had so successfully managed a first show. The second vice-president and the chairman of nomenclature was Mr. Holley of Cromwell, Connecticut, whose previous work on saintpaulias at the University of New Hampshire had already brought him coast-to-coast recognition. Mrs. Robert Wright of Knoxville, Tennessee, became secretary. She has organized two African violet clubs and also has charge of the first bulletins. Lewis E. Cook, of Gainesville, New York is the corresponding secretary. Boyce M. Edens of Atlanta was elected treasurer. He helped with the first show and has many African violets. The charter members came from twenty states.

On this memorable occasion of the first show a local group of enthusiasts also organized as the Greater Atlanta African Violet Society. Mrs. G. E. Rhodes of Atlanta was installed as the first president with Mrs. J. M. B. Bloodworth, Mrs. Marie L. Mann, and Mrs. L. R. Jessie as other officers. Since all these people are part of the African violet's history it seems fitting to record them here in this, the African violet's first book!

Problems of Classification

The work of the Classification Committee has been most difficult and the members deserve the thanks of every devotee of the saintpaulia. In my own investigations I have discovered such a mass of contradiction and duplication that I have wondered how one simple plant in fifty years could have plunged into so much confusion. A variety of well-defined name and characteristics in the East may not apparently exist in the West until a letter from a western hobbyist brings news of a plant with exactly the same color of flower and shape of leaf but, alas, with an entirely different name. Such matters have given both the committee and me a special variety of saintpaulia headache which leads me at least to make my first descriptive list of varieties in a spirit of considerable humility. (Perhaps, too, I have been conditioned by my earlier work with the centuries-old geranium and its even greater confusions.)

In any case organization will help us all. We will appreciate membership in the new society and be glad to abide by show rules which require us to enter named plants of a given age so that their characteristics may be considered fairly "fixed" and to name plants as "new" only after the society recognizes them as such. Meanwhile at clubs, societies, and shows we will enjoy meeting many unknown saintpaulia "friends" and comparing notes with them. Indeed, I am not at all sure that the African violet's greatest excuse for being is not its already proven ability to foster friendship among its enthusiasts!

APPLICATION FOR MEMBERSHIP IN THE AFRICAN VIOLET SOCIETY OF AMERICA, INC.

Mr. Boyce M. Edens, *Treasurer*
2694 Lenox Road, N.E.   ...., 19....
Atlanta, Georgia.

Please enroll me as a .... member of the African Violet Society of America, Inc. I enclose the amount checked below as my dues for a twelve month period.

RECOMMENDED BY   Signed ....
                      Street Address ....
....   City and State...............

CHECK THE CLASS OF MEMBERSHIP WANTED
Individual Member (January 1 to December 31), $3.00.
Sustaining Member (Commercial) (January 1 to December 31), $10.00.
Make Checks Payable to the African Violet Society of America, Inc.

Back:

AFRICAN VIOLET SOCIETY OF AMERICA, INC.

ARTICLE II—BY-LAWS

OBJECT

Its object shall be—

1. The purpose of this organization shall be both educational and scientific in that one may be able to enlarge the groups of those interested in this plant.

2. To properly arrange, to classify the many varieties as to color, leaf character, growth, etc.

3. This organization shall be ready to assist in promoting the growth of and to encourage the propagation of new and better varieties.

4. To work out proper methods of disease control and all other matters that may be of interest to the members.

5. It shall hold meetings at which times methods and demonstration, growth, and fertilization and all other activities connected with this plant shall be discussed.

6. Bulletins shall be issued to the members, and reports of its officers be submitted for approval of the membership.

CHAPTER TEN

Packing, and Sources of Supply

FROM MY rather extensive observation, I believe I can state as fact that there never was or will be an African violet enthusiast who can be content with two or three varieties. When first I made the acquaintance of this gem of a plant, I thought the blossoms of the species so utterly beautiful that I could see no possible reason for wanting other colors. To my regret I recall stating in print, some ten years ago perhaps, that pink African violets seemed unnecessary to me when we already had such glowing purples.

Now I take it all back. In the face of Pink Beauty or duPont Lavender Pink I am truly apologetic. Let us have violets in all possible shades, I think now, for the loveliness of a purple, lavender, rose, and white collection at a window is, indeed, not to be equalled by a one-color display.

The inexpensive way to achieve variety is to swap leaves with other collectors or to buy leaves from growers who sell them as well as the rooted plants. You can then propagate for yourself and slowly but surely develop an extensive representation. When leaves are exchanged, the aim is to pack them so that they can travel well through the mails to great distances. They should arrive in such fresh condition that full vitality remains to nourish a new crop of plants.

Wrapping Leaves

When preparing leaves for mailing, you will find it a good plan to wrap the entire leaf stem in moist sphagnum moss (the florist uses this extensively for packing) or in damp peat moss. Enfold the leaf itself loosely but completely with dry excelsior or a piece of facial tissue. Enclose the entire protected leaf then in a stiff layer of wax paper.

Fasten the leaf to a section of strong corrugated paper and place the whole thing in a cardboard box. Finally wrap, tie, and label for parcel post or first-class mailing. First class is more expensive, of course, but also quicker and in this transaction speed is of the essence. The trick is to keep the leaves as short a time as possible out of a growing medium of water or soil and in transit to maintain moist stems and dry tops. It is also important to prevent any shifting of the leaf during the journey. Wrapping must be thick enough to protect leaves from crushing in handling and particularly when the box is stamped. In warm weather holes should be punched in the heavier coverings to provide some means of ventilation.

Zoning Regulations

Whether you live in a quarantined Japanese beetle zone or not does not matter when only leaves are involved. If whole plants are being mailed or shipped, they are not permitted to go out of quarantined zones into beetle-free zones except after inspection, unless every bit of soil is first washed from the roots. You can get more specific information on zoning by writing to the Bureau of Plant Quarantine, Department of Agriculture, in your own state. At the present time, I learn from the national Department of Agriculture that either the whole or part of the following states are in quarantined zones: Connecticut, Delaware, District of Columbia, Maine, Maryland, Massachusetts, New Hampshire, New Jersey, New York, Ohio, Pennsylvania, Rhode Island, Vermont, Virginia, and West Virginia.

Mailing *into* quarantined zones poses no problem. It is the outgoing carriers of the dreaded Japanese beetle pest which the government is so justifiably interested in.

Wrapping Plants

The successful wrapping of plants for a short or long carry has been beautifully worked out by a number of responsible growers. Indeed, I have marveled at the care and skill with which well-grown plants have been so handled that they have come to me in absolutely perfect condition, ready to go on and grow at my windows without ever "missing a beat." Considering the brittleness of stem and leaf I congratulate the careful packers.

One firm in particular does an unusually good job of packing. In a carton three inches in diameter and twelve inches long I received a plant with an eight-inch leaf spread! It successfully carried two blooms and nine buds and the foliage, released from its upright position, spread out unmarred.

The base of the plant, that is the paper pot and soil, was packed in a lint substance held by string wound twice around and underneath the pot. Two thicknesses of brown paper, with a quarter-inch insulating layer of the same linty material between them, were then wrapped around the whole, the leaves being carefully drawn upwards to fit eventual carton size. Around this first packing was a piece of tin foil with a yellow ribbon holding it! Then came three sheets of newspaper tied with string, top and bottom.

The packaged plant was next slipped into a cylindrical cardboard carton with a label and directions for growing included. Finally all was fitted into an oblong corrugated carton which was wrapped and labeled for mailing.

I do not claim that such an elaborate system of packing is necessary but I can vouch for its effectiveness. Since the firm which goes to these careful lengths handles quantities of plants, I judge they have discovered that such precautions are worth what they undoubtedly must cost in labor and materials.

A less complicated method is employed by another successful grower. She packs the plant roots in moist sphagnum moss, and wraps the entire plant first in waxed paper and then in heavy cardboard with two perforations near the bottom, where the plant roots rest. Around the waxed paper she winds string with long enough ends to draw through the perforations in the first wrapping of cardboard. She ties these ends of string firmly on the outside of the cardboard.

The name of the plant is clearly written on this first stiff wrapper. The package is next placed on a bed of shredded and crumpled newspaper in a reinforced cardboard box of the type used for loaf cheese. The string from the center is again pulled through perforations in the final outside wrapping and tied firmly around this covering so as to anchor the plant securely for the duration of its journey. Anyone will find these materials readily at hand and can confidently send plants so protected.

Where to Buy

In so far as it is possible, it is a good plan to secure your plants in seasons of cool weather. Indeed, most firms do not attempt hot-weather mailings. It is also wise to buy saintpaulias from a local rather than a distant grower. African violets are so succulent in growth and their stems so brittle that extended journeys are always hazardous for them. Packaged seeds, of course, are to be purchased whenever they are available.

You may depend on the following retail firms to take every reasonable precaution with the packing and shipping of plants. From many of them either my friends or I have received orders, so that I can personally vouch for them. All others have been recommended to me by those whose judgment and disinterestedness I feel I can rely on.

Inquiries to growers should always be accompanied by

a self-addressed, stamped envelope for reply. These people are overwhelmed by correspondence so that it is only kind to simplify their task as much as possible.

Barnes, Mrs. Pansy M. 206 E. Summit Street, Shenandoah, Iowa.

Baxter, R. G., 2023 Belmont Avenue, Youngstown 4, Ohio.

Brown, Mrs. R. A., 55 Wesley Avenue, Newnan, Georgia.

Burrell Gardens, 19 Elgin Street, St. Thomas, Ontario, Canada.

Friendly Gardens, New Bedford, Pennsylvania (Seeds and leaves only).

Glen St. Mary Nurseries, Glen St. Mary, Florida.

Gregg and Pease Gardens, Zumbrota, Minnesota.

McGregor Brothers Co., Springfield, Ohio.

Salzer Seed Co., J. A., La Crosse, Wisconsin.

Starr Dahlia Gardens, 869 Confederate Avenue S. E. Atlanta, Georgia.

Tinari Floral Garden, Valley Road, Bethayres, Pennsylvania.

Virginia Lee Gardens, Greensboro, Maryland.

CHAPTER ELEVEN

Classification of Varieties

NOT SO LONG ago there was but one African violet, a species, known to the initiated as Saintpaulia ionantha. Then came a few fine purples like Blue Boy. In recent years a pink and a white appeared, but matters kept within bounds and the enthusiast with some ten varieties had pretty well covered the field.

But behold the situation today. Before me is a listing of more than one hundred and seventy-five names of varieties. Doubtless there are duplications here. Doubtless, too, there are other varieties of which I have not yet heard. To my personal knowledge, however, there are seventy-four varieties, all seen with my own eyes, all differing, though some in very minor ways, all separately named, and most of them in the collection belonging to Mrs. Freed. Considering the present interest in hybridizing and also the tendency of the plant to sport, I cannot imagine what the rabid collector of the future may attempt to encompass!

Definite strains as well as varieties are appearing. Any variety may, for instance, develop what are termed du-Pont, Supreme, Leatherneck, or Amazon characteristics. (The variety Supreme, just to be contrary, does not have the qualities of the Supreme strain, and is an instance of unfortunate nomenclature.) The Supreme strain is characterized by unusual brittleness of foliage.

The duPont strain is characterized by thick, hairy, quilted leaves, somewhat curled and with a pie-crust edge. It is slow-growing, not very prolific, but when in bloom produces very large flowers crowded on just a few stems.

The Leatherneck strain, developed by R. A. Brown in Georgia, is characterized by smooth leaf edges and flexible growth, which, being pliable, travels better.

The Amazons, also from the Browns, are very like the duPont strain but the Browns report that the leaves incline "to cup down slightly and in the blue series the leaf edges are dentate."

Varieties cannot be so simply dealt with, but the Classification Committee of the African Violet Society strives under Mr. Holley's direction for clarification and I, after many inspections of collections, many meetings, and a correspondence, which I can only describe as monumental, offer this first assembling of data. It is not meant to be final and only as authoritative as my present knowledge permits.

Colors and Groups

Colors are indicated according to a chart which has been developed from an *actual sequence* of flowers picked from plants in full bloom and arranged on a table according to gradation of color. On any chart, however, color designation can be only tentative, since hues vary on the same variety, and sometimes even on the same plant. Saintpaulia colors depend considerably on the amount of light to which plants are exposed, the kind of soil in which they grow, and even according to the season of the year.

Arrangement in five major classifications by color seems to me a practical procedure for identifying African violets. For quick reference I am therefore placing varieties, as I know them, somewhat according to the plan worked out by the first show committee at Atlanta, but with certain changes which my own research suggested as practical. I am also indicating five supplementary groups of Doubles, Bicolors, Miniatures, Variegateds, and Novelties, with all varieties in these groups also included in the five major classifications. *However, when varieties show unfixed tendencies to characteristics of doubleness, bicoloration, limited size, or leaf variegation, they are classified by color only.*

The same attitude holds for albinos, since such plants lack vitality and do not survive as fixed varieties. Plants frequently develop an all-white stalk or a few all-white leaves, but there is usually little stamina or longevity in this section of growth.

Regarding the to-date non-existent yellows, enough, perhaps too much, has already been said. Saintpaulias are highly unlikely to produce such hues since they evidently belong to that class of plants which lack the essential elements for the production of yellow. Here is the scientific basis for color in flowers as it is explained by Holman and Robbins in *A Textbook of General Botany*:

In the cells of beet roots and of the flowers, leaves, or other parts of many plants, the cell sap frequently contains dissolved anthocyanin pigments which give them a red, purple, or blue color. The anthocyanins belong to a chemical group known as the glucosides; these are compounds which, when broken up into less complex substances, yield the sugar glucose, or some other monosacharose, and certain other compounds. The reaction of the cell sap determines the color of the anthocyanins: for example, when the cell sap is alkaline, the color is blue, and when the cell sap is acid, the color is red. The function of anthocyanins is still a matter of dispute.

In the carrot, on the other hand, the yellow color is due to pigments in the chromoplasts. In some flowers the two methods of coloration are combined, both colored cell sap and chromoplasts being found in the same cell."

The chromoplasts, which are present in many cells, are specialized bodies, spherical or ellipsoidal in shape, which are part of the cytoplasm and float in it. They are of three kinds: the colorless leucoplasts; the green chloroplasts, containing chlorophyll; and the chromoplasts with yellow, orange, red, or brown pigments, as carotene and xanthophyll.

Here then is the alignment by color as it appears in the chart:

SAINT PAULIA

White	
White Lady	

BV. 6 Pale Blue Violet	V. 6 Pale Lavender
Sky Blue	
BV. 5 Very Light Blue Violet	V. 5 Light Lavender
Blue Eyes	
BV. 4 Light Blue Violet	V. 4 Lavender
S. ionantha	Myrtle

BV. 3 Medium Blue Violet	V. 3 Medium Purple
du Pont Blue	
BV. 2 Blue Violet	V. 2 Purple
Blue Boy	Mentor
BV. 1 Intense Blue Violet	V. 1 Intense Purple
Viking	Purple Prince

Five classifications in a comparative color sequence based on actual flower tint gradations of freshly picked blossoms. Numbers 1, 2, 3, indicate deeper colors;

COLOR CHART

White
White Lady

CLASS III	CLASS IV
RV.6 Pale Lavender Pink	R.6 Pale Pink
	Blushing Maiden
RV.5 Light Lavender Pink	R.5 Light Pink
du Pont Lavender Pink	Blush Beauty
RV.4 Lavender Pink	R.4 Pink
Plum	Pink Beauty
RV.3 Medium Red Violet	R.3 Rose
Orchid Girl	
RV.2 Red Violet	R.2 Carmine
RV.1 Intense Red Violet	R.1 Intense Carmine
Red Bicolor, upper part	

CLASS III   **CLASS IV**

4, 5, 6, indicate paler tints, fading to 7, or white. Some color sections still lack available representative varieties.

Class I. Purple, Medium, and Dark Blue-Violet.

Class II. Lavender and Light Blue-Violet. Varieties placed in this group always show *more blue than pink* in the flowers.

Class III. Red-Violet. Varieties placed in this group always show *more pink than blue*. Here will be included so-called reds. I have never seen any saintpaulias of a bright flag red, although I have been told about them. The reds I know are burgundy or red-wine colors. And no fixed division is made here of light and dark Red-Violets as is made with Blue-Violets and Lavenders. The reason is that saintpaulias in the red-violet range are much more variable and unfixed in their degrees of lightness and darkness.

Class IV. Pink. Here there will undoubtedly be disagreement, especially in regards to a variety like duPont Lavender Pink which by name would be placed here, but by actual color is more accurately located in Class III.

Class V. White. This is an obvious and therefore most welcome classification.

Here is the alignment according to certain other considerations:

Group A. Doubles. This includes varieties which are fixed in their ability to regularly produce flowers of twelve to seventeen petals. Many saintpaulias like Viking increase the number of petals beyond five, but the tendency is not really fixed. Double Russian, introduced in 1947, belongs in Group A (also in Class I) since reproduced vegetatively over a period of time, it has continued to offer only double flowers. Double Russian is

Pink; as Large, up to one and three-fourths inches, as in Blue Boy; as Medium, up to one and one-half inches, as in White Lady; as Small, up to one and one-fourth inches, as in Blue Eyes.

Originators of varieties are indicated where known but attempts should not be made to obtain plants from them. Place your orders with regular retail growers. There is a limited list of these sources given in Chapter X.

In the following descriptions is included all information available to me to date. In the case of a variety not known to me, I have indicated the source of the description given. Through subsequent editions of this book classification will be extended, as it is possible, or even altered. At this point I certainly do not claim infallibility —only honesty. Perhaps also I should admit to considerable temerity that in the face of so many claimants and so much controversy, some of which almost approaches violence, I offer to a none too peaceful world further cause for disagreement.

Classification by Color

Class I

Purple, Medium, and Dark Blue-Violet

BLUE BIRD
Flower. Medium, blue-violet with long, tapered petals. Large and flaring blossom suggests a bird. B.V.3.
Leaf. Large, medium green, slightly ribbed, and rosy beneath. Medium petioles. Similar to Blue Boy.
Plant. Upright growth and very attractive.
Originated: Charles Merkel and Sons, Ohio.

BLUE BOY (*Illustrated*)
Flower. Deep blue-violet. Large and rather flat and prolific, appearing among and above leaves. Petioles dark red. B.V.2.
Leaf. Ovate with small regular crenations, rather flat with edges curled down, sometimes bent. Light dull green above, pale below. Petiole pinkish, drooping, horizontal or upright to a thirty-degree angle.
Plant. Fine and handsome. Excellent bloomer. Growth thick, even bunchy.
Originated: Armacost and Royston, California.

Blue Boy

BLUE BOY SUPREME (*Illustrated*)

Flower. Deep blue-violet with broad petals like a duPont. Extra large and held slightly above foliage in tight clusters. B.V.2.

Leaf. Broad, ovate, obtuse with large regular scallops. Dull green above, noticeably pored, coarse, and thick though not particularly lumpy between veins. Margins curl down (convex) and are irregularly bent. Light green below. Petioles horizontal and pinkish.

Plant. Pleasing flattish plant, somewhat like duPont Blue but leaves incline to be longer and petioles shorter.

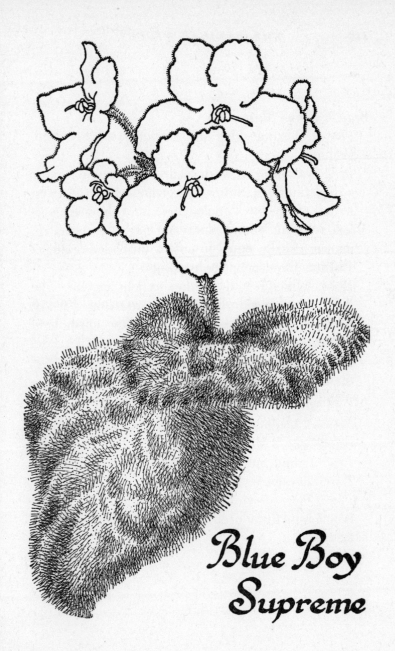

Blue Boy Supreme

BLUE CHARD (*Illustrated*)

Flower. Medium blue and medium-sized. Set deep. Prolific.

Leaf. Narrow-ovate, with small crenation and usually a rippled margin. Shiny dark green above, pale green to dull rose below. Petioles curve up with some leaves held vertical. Young plants are not so exaggerated; petioles usually raised to only a thirty-degree angle. Position also depends on exposure.

Plant. Unique with striking upright growth. The dark wavy foliage forms a nest in the center of which blossoms usually open much below the upper level of leaves.

Named and Introduced: Friendly Gardens and Virginia Lee Gardens.

BLUE FLUTE (Formerly duPont Blue Flute)

Flower. Medium blue. Slightly rippled or crimped petal edges. B.V.3.

Leaf. Round and convex with edges curled down. Dark olive-green.

Plant. Slow growing.

Named and Introduced: Tinari Floral Gardens, Pennsylvania.

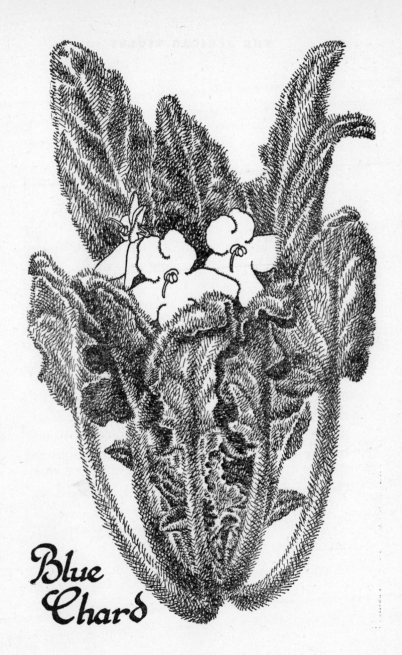

Blue
Chard

BLUE GIRL (*Illustrated*)

Flower. Deep, blue-violet. Cupped and large. Held slightly above leaves on a rosy stem. Prolific B.V.2.

Leaf. Broad-cordate and obtuse. Young leaves deeply crenate with large, sometimes twisted and overlapping segments. Scallops seem to grow more shallow as leaf ages. Light green above, with a large irregular pale spot at leaf base, and a tiny pale spot at base (sinus) of each scallop. Pale below. Pinkish petioles upright at a thirty- to forty-five-degree angle.

Plant. Beautiful upright grower with variegation. Plants vary considerably from those with little scalloping or spotting to those which are so distinctive that the margins of mature leaves are irregularly pinched back upon themselves. Even old leaves may be true to form, the pale spot remaining large and definite. Sport of Blue Boy.

Originated: Ulery Greenhouses, Ohio. Patented.

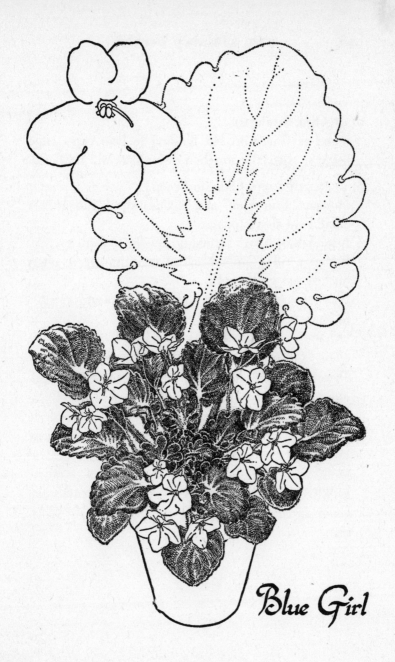

Blue Girl

BLUE GIRL SUPREME
Same as Blue Girl but tending to bear extra large
flowers, especially so when disbudded and fertilized.

BLUE SCOOP (syn. Chicago Scoop)
Flower. "True blue" and medium-sized. Bloom in a
circle held above foliage.
Leaf. Young leaves turned up at edge to form a scoop.
Rather a slick, quilted leaf of medium green, often
flushed red underneath.
Plant. Charming variety of "the Neptune group."
Growth is flat and of rosette form.
Originated (and described by): Jane Coleman. Syn-
onym occurred when plant, first called Scoop because
of leaf form, was grown by a Chicago enthusiast.

COMMANDER (See page 178)
Flower. Dark purple and large.
Leaf. Large, slick, dark green, pointed leaf "well .
patterned."
Plant. One of the handsomest. Known to have been
grown in Garfield Park Conservatory in Chicago
about fifteen years ago. (Described by Jane Coleman.)

CRINKLES

Flower. Medium violet and shaped like Neptune. Medium-sized. B.V.3.

Leaf. Dark green with light green stripe running partway along midrib from base. Margins with shallow scallops. Sometimes wavy or rippled. Convex or humped and dark red below.

Plant. Attractive and unusual appearance. Growth rippled and slightly drooping.

Named and Introduced: Tinari Floral Gardens, Pennsylvania.

CURLY SPECIAL

Flower. Same as Blue Girl though may be misshapen and often asymmetrical. B.V. 2.

Leaf. Recognizable scalloping of Blue Girl but twisted and contorted to an almost grotesque extent. (Probably due to some virus.) Petioles very short.

Plant. Bunchy appearance, not particularly pleasing. Originated: Lauches Greenhouses, Beaver Falls, Pennsylvania.

DOUBLE BLUE BOY (See page 178)

Flower. Same color and form as Duchess. Less intense than Blue Boy because paler petal reverses are much in evidence and weaken hue. About fifteen petals. V.2.

Leaf. Typical Blue Boy foliage, with tiny dark surface veins. Lighter yellow-green than foliage of other doubles with dark blue flowers.

Plant. Undistinguished manner of growth.

Originated: Ulery Greenhouses, Ohio, (subsequently dropped by them).

DOUBLE RUSSIAN (*Illustrated*) (See page 178)

Flower. Purple. Small and double with fourteen to seventeen petals per bloom. Petals whitish below, cupped when young, usually taking a week to open fully into a more or less regular pompom. No stamens in evidence. Stems rather dark. V.2

Leaf. Dull, light green, suggests Blue Boy.

Plant. Low growing, not over four inches including flowers which are interesting but not beautiful.

Introduced: Tinari Floral Gardens, Pennsylvania. (1946)

Double
Russian

DUCHESS (Probably Double Blue Boy. See page 178)
Flower. Purple. Small and double with from nine to thirteen petals in irregular formation. Undersides almost white and usually much in evidence. Prolific. V.2
Leaf. Dull green, small, on short petiole. Crowded. Leaves and flowers not over three inches in height.
Plant. Apparently same as Double Russian.
Named and Introduced: Jennie Spoutz, Michigan.

DuPONT BLUE (*Illustrated*)
Flower. Light violet. Extra large with broad round petals. Flowers in rather stiff clusters open at level of tallest leaves. B.V.3
Leaf. Almost round with fairly deep and regularly scalloped edge, curled down. Light dull green with long hairs above, pale below. Pinkish petioles not quite horizontal to thirty-degree angle.
Plant. Lovely, with growth flat to convex and very effective flowering. Slow growing.
Originated: Mrs. William K. duPont, Delaware.

MENTOR BOY (See also Purple Mist)
Flower. Violet-purple. Large. Stems dark red and rather long. Prolific. V.2
Leaf. Ovate. Bright green with margins slightly turned down. Pale green to faint rose below. Petioles long and held at a thirty-degree angle.
Plant. Attractive and valuable for free-blooming nature.
Originated: Charles Merkel and Sons, Ohio.

du Pont Blue

NEPTUNE

Flower. Blue violet. Medium-sized. Short stems. Blooms among and slightly above leaves. B.V.3

Leaf. Ovate, broadly acute, slightly troughed and cupped at base with large, shallow, regular crenations. Shiny, dark olive-green above, white to rosy below.

Plant. Flat with overlapping leaves and short-petioled flowers set close among them.

Originated: Armacost and Royston, California.

NEPTUNE SPOONED or NEPTUNE IMPROVED (*Illustrated*)

Flower. Same as Neptune. B.V.3

Leaf. Resembles Neptune but sometimes obovate (broadest above middle), quilted between veins, thick, and so deeply cupped (concave) that almost as much of the underside of the leaf shows as the upper surface.

Plant. Flat and shiny, and often quite dark.

NORSEMAN

Flower. A medium, exquisite blue, and large. Petals round. Short stems. B.V.3

Leaf. Blunt-ovate, dark shiny green with light green stripe running halfway along midrib from base. Rose to dark rose below, depending on exposure.

Plant. Flat and dark, very appealing variety.

Originated: Armacost and Royston, California.

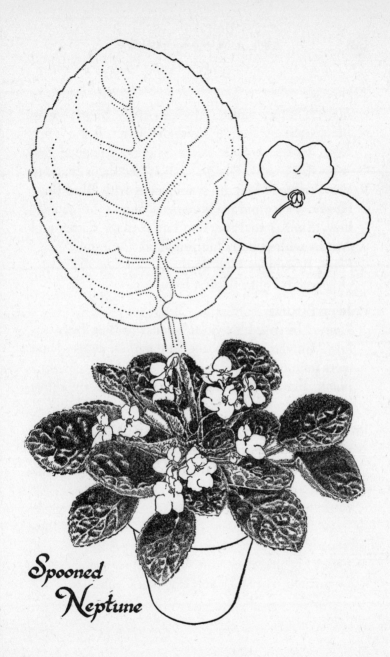

Spooned
Neptune

PANSY PURPLE (May be synonymous with Blue Boy)
Flower. Violet and medium-sized. V.2
Leaf. Similar to Blue Boy but perhaps flatter and thinner with petioles horizontal.
Plant. Resembles Blue Boy.
Originated: Pansy Barnes, Iowa.

PURPLE BEAUTY
Flower. Intense blue-violet, similar to Blue Boy.
Leaf. Similar to Neptune but darker, longer, and more pointed leaf.
Plant. Similar to Neptune. (Described by Alma Wright)

PURPLE MIST (May be synonymous with Mentor Boy)
Flower. Violet-purple. V.2
Leaf. Somewhat larger than Mentor Boy.

Purple Prince
Flower. Rich, clear purple. Medium-sized. Prolific.
V.1
Leaf. Light green, flat, and pointed.
Plant. Pleasing but not unusual.
Originated: R. G. Baxter, Ohio (1947).

Rose Purple
Flower. Violet-purple. Large. Long petioles standing well above leaves. Prolific.
Leaf. Large, medium to dark green and red underneath. Oval shape with sharp point, heavily veined, slightly serrated. Petioles long and inclined to grow in rosette formation, with leaves slightly cupped down over container. Propagates easily. (Described by Mrs. F. L. Beers, Georgia)

SAPPHIRE (*Illustrated*)

Flower. Light blue-violet. Lower three petals well separated and all five turned back slightly. Margins irregular. Medium-sized. B.V.3

Leaf. Ovate-cordate, blunt. Flat, with small regular crenation. Shiny, green above, almost white to rosy below. Long pinkish petioles, more or less upright to thirty-degree angle or more, depending on exposure.

Plant. Similar to Neptune of which it is a seedling. "A good house plant but a poor commercial variety." Originated: W. D. Holley, New Hampshire.

SUPREME (May be synonymous with Viking and Admiral)

Flower. Rich purple, shaped like Viking. Medium-sized. Held well above leaves. Prolific. B.V.1

Leaf. Ovate, troughed, dark green above and rosy to cabbage-red below. Petioles horizontal.

Plant. Pleasing and free flowering. Not of Supreme strain. Slow growing.

THIRTY-TWO "32"

Flower. Medium blue-violet, medium-sized on long stems well above foliage. B.V.3

Leaf. Acutely tapered tip, cordate base. Medium petioles. Medium satiny green. Smooth, rose-tinted below with much darker veins.

Plant. Growth develops into a flat rosette. Originated: Armacost and Royston, California. (Described by Mrs. Arthur Radtke)

Sapphire

Topaz

Flower. Medium blue-violet and medium-sized with dark petioles sometimes shorter than leaf stems. Amethyst form but of a somewhat darker shade with petals sometimes curled back. B.V.3

Leaf. Ovate to cordate and troughed. Olive green and rosy below with green veins. Petioles long, upright to thirty-degree angle.

Plant. Attractive and of variable growth with flowers held among leaves. Distinguished from Sapphire by darker flowers, stems, leaves, and petioles.

Originated: W. D. Holley, New Hampshire.

Turquoise

Flower. Medium blue. Calyx and stems dark purple. B.V.3

Leaf. Round-ovate with small scalloping. Dark bronzy green above and noticeably dark red below with light green veins. Petioles rosy and very long.

Plant. Attractive, olive-green.

Originated: W. D. Holley, New Hampshire.

Viking (*Illustrated*)

Flower. Blue-violet deeper than Blue Boy, slightly purple on margins. Medium-sized. Flat rounded petals showing tendency to double to eight. B.V.1

Leaf. Ovate, acute, with regular small crenations slightly troughed. Dark olive-green above, deep rose below, veins and all. Petioles rosy, almost horizontal.

Plant. Flat, spreading, and dark green. Prolific.

Originated: Armacost and Royston, California.

Viking

Class II

Lavender and Light Blue-Violet

AMETHYST (*Illustrated*)

Flower. Blue-lavender of individual shape with almost horizontal side petals, the lowest one long, the two upper ones well separated from the lower three. Medium-sized and held well above leaves. Prolific. B.V.4

Leaf. Ovate, acute, with small regular crenations. Thick, troughed, and slightly cupped at base. Dark olive-green above with small whitish spot at leaf base. Below quite rosy between the veins. Petiole rosy, horizontal, and stiff.

Plant. Beautiful, spreading grower with pleasing contrast of dark leaves and light flowers.

Originated: William Palmer and Sons. Named: Armacost and Royston, California.

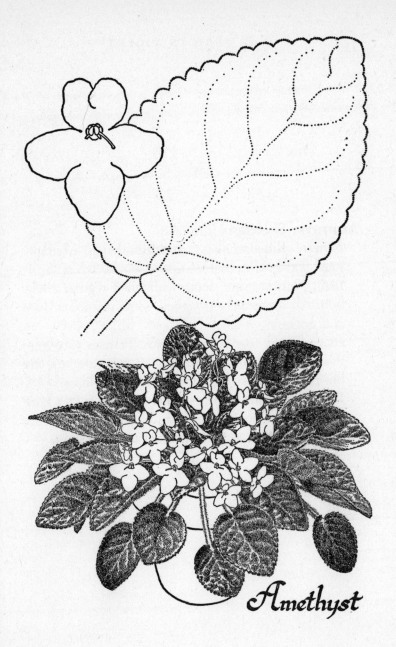

Amethyst

AMETHYST SPOONED (*Illustrated*)

Flower. Blue-lavender, Amethyst-shape. Medium-sized and held as high as tips of leaves. B.V.4

Leaf. Narrow-ovate, acute with small regular crenation. All leaves very troughed, some cupped at base and enclosing a small light spot. Shiny, olive-green above. Below rosy between veins. Petioles vary from two to three inches, depending on exposure, and are horizontal to upright at thirty-degree angle.

Plant. Sometimes appears spidery. Varies from a horizontal and drooping appearance, when petioles are long, to a stiff upright look when they are short.

Spooned
Amethyst

BLUE EYES (*Illustrated*)

Flower. Pale blue-lavender. The nearest of any saint-paulia to a true, pale, sky blue. Petals usually curved back. Small, in close clusters of a few flowers held well above leaves. B.V.5

Leaf. Ovate, acute, thick, with small regular crenation. Young leaves are dark green, shiny, troughed, and lumpy. Older leaves become flat, dull, dusty looking. Below, only veins are pinkish. Petioles almost horizontal.

Plant. A flat rosette type, desirable for unique paleness of flowers.

Introduced: Tinari Floral Gardens, Pennsylvania.

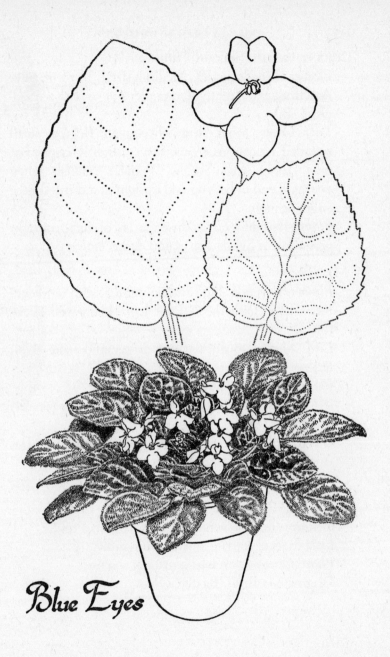

Blue Eyes

IONANTHA, THE SPECIES (*Illustrated*)

Flower. Blue-lavender. Medium-sized, like a smaller Amethyst but slightly darker, yet not so dark as Sapphire. B.V.4

Leaf. Ovate, acute, shiny olive-green. Regular small rounded crenations. Some leaves slightly cupped at base. Light green below. Petioles pinkish when young. Tend to be long and upright at a thirty-degree angle or more.

Plant. Resembles Amethyst but is of more upright growth with lighter leaves and darker flowers.

MARINE

Flower. Lavender-blue and lighter than duPont Blue. Extra large with the duPont look. Held well above foliage.

Leaf. Similar to duPont but darker and more rigid. Rather quilted.

Plant. Unusually large spreading rosette. Most pleasing. Considered finest of all varieties by some collectors.

Originated (and described by): Clarissa Harris, Los Angeles (1940). Blue Boy X S. ionantha.

MYRTLE

Flower. "Periwinkle" blue. Rather long stems holding medium-sized flowers well above plant. Prolific. V.4

Leaf. Round-cordate and medium green.

Plant. Growth develops into a flat rosette.

Originated: R. G. Baxter, Ohio.

S. ionantha

Orchid Flute
Flower. Lavender with bicolor tendency. Upper two petals darker (V.4) and lower ones quite pale (V.6). Minutely scalloped and crimped margin of petals shows very narrow edge of darker color. Usual du-Pont size and shape. V.4 and V.6
Leaf. DuPont type.
Plant. Handsome and desirable. Slow growing.
Named and Introduced: Tinari Floral Gardens, Pennsylvania.

Ruffles (*Illustrated*)
Flower. Medium blue-lavender. Lower three petals well separated from upper two. Middle petal unusually long. Flower sometimes asymmetrical and held well above all but the new leaves. Medium-sized. Often doubles to eight petals. Stems very dark. B.V.4
Leaf. Narrow-ovate and troughed with margin irregularly scalloped and rippled. Shiny, dark, olive-green above, rosy below. Petioles rosy and horizontal but with mature leaves drooping.
Plant. Charming and low growing. An interesting variation among saintpaulias with some plants much more ruffled or rippled than others. Slow growing.
Named and Introduced: Elsie C. Freed, Pennsylvania (1945).

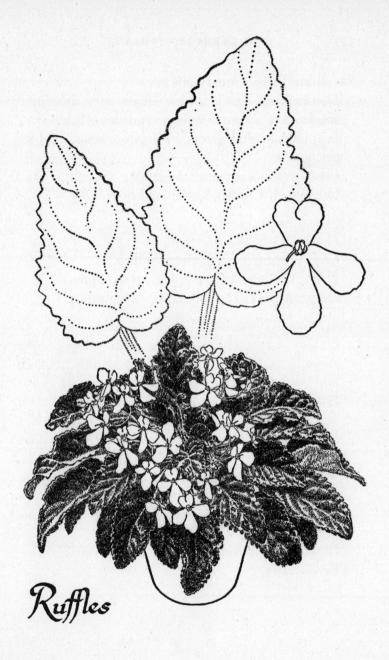

Ruffles

SKY BLUE (syn. Tinted Lady)
Flower. Pale blue-lavender, almost grey. Medium-sized and of a shape similar to Amethyst. B.V.6
Leaf. Small, dull green. Pale green below. Petiole pale green.
Plant. Resembles a small Amethyst.
Originated: Charles Merkel and Sons, Ohio.

SUMMER SKIES
Flower. Light violet.
Leaf. Very light green, almost yellow.
Plant. The bunchy White-Lady type of growth.
Originated: W. D. Holley, New Hampshire.

WATERLILY (*Illustrated*) (syn. Starlight)
Flower. Light, blue-lavender with deeper color around center. Small and cupped slightly. Shaped like Viking. Held above leaves. Stems dark. B.V.4
Leaf. Broad-ovate, very shallow crenation. Rather dusty grey-green above with white margins showing on underside. Deep rose below. Very thin young leaves cupped and slightly ruffled. Old ones quite flat with edges turned up (concave) suggesting foliage of a waterlily.
Plant. Rather slow growing. Interesting, unique appearance. Flat and grey.
Named and Introduced: Mrs. Robert Wright, Tennessee (1947).

Waterlily

Class III

Red-Violet

COMMANDO

Flower. Wine-red. Large.
Leaf. Very large foliage.
Plant. A sport of the Mentor Boy family.
Named and Introduced: V. S. Starr, Georgia. (Described by Jane Coleman)

COMMODORE (See page 178)

Flower. Reddish-purple. Large.
Leaf. Pointed and slick. Dark green to reddish-black. Similar to Viking, except that growth is flatter.
Plant. Sturdy and excellent type. One of the oldest named varieties. (Described by Jane Coleman)

DuPONT AMETHYST

Flower. Lavender-pink, more uniform coloring and pinker than duPont Lavender Pink. Fine, dark line around petal margins. Large. R.V.5
Leaf. Usual duPont, quilted type.
Plant. Flat rosette type of growth. Slow growing.

DuPONT LAVENDER PINK (Originally duPont Pink, *Illustrated*)

Flower. Pale lavender with bicolor tendency. Young flowers and the two upper petals of mature blooms usually darker. Held above leaves in stiff, close clusters. Extra large. Petals broad with irregular edges. R.V.5
Leaf. Broad-ovate, almost round and regularly scal-

du Pont
Lavender Pink

loped. Large and flat with a quilted look. Older leaves
with margins curled down. Dull green, pored, with
long hairs above. Pale below. Pinkish petioles horizontal to slightly raised.

Plant. A flat spreading type. One of the loveliest of all
saintpaulias and the favorite of many collectors. Slow
growing.

Originated: Mrs. William K. duPont.

DWARF ORCHID BEAUTY

Flower. The same as Orchid Beauty. R.V.4

Leaf. Tiny flat rosette, mottled olive-yellow and
green.

Plant. Pleasing in this smaller edition of Orchid
Beauty.

FRIEDA (May be synonymous with Red or Pink Ionan-
tha)

Flower. Dark red-violet. Medium-sized and held close
to leaves. R.V.2

Leaf. Dark green, shiny, and slightly cupped. Veins
prominent, Reddish below. Tapered tips and small
crenation. Long petioles.

Plant. Rather compact rosette. (Described by Mrs.
Arthur Radtke)

Originated: Ulery Greenhouses, Ohio.

GORGEOUS

Flower. Orchid-rose, darker than Orchid Beauty and
pinker, but flowers of somewhat the same shape.
Small. R.V.3

Leaf. Ovate, acute, and decidedly cupped or shell-shaped, and pointed. Medium green. Light rose, pale veins below. Petioles raised to thirty-degree angle.

Plant. Pleasing with a nest of pointed, spooned leaves.

Originated: R. G. Baxter, Ohio. Patent pending.

Lilac Lady

Flower. Pale lavender-pink. Same color and shape as Orchid Beauty, but considerably smaller. R.V.4

Leaf. Flat and dark green, shaped like Amethyst.

Plant. Miniature growth. Roots slowly. Probably a sport of Amethyst.

Mary Wac (See page 178)

Flower. Violet-red with darker markings from center to tip. Shows slight bicolor tendency with two upper petals darker. Coloring varies in degree of intensity as in all plants of this violet-red group. Sometimes throws a solid lilac bloom on the same cluster with violet-red flowers. R.V.4

Leaf. Medium to dark green. Ovate with slightly dentate edge. Petioles and veins reddish on underside. Slightly hairy.

Plant. Drooping growth like Plum.

Originated: R. A. Brown, Georgia.

My Second Prize

Flower. Rose-purple of medium size. Prolific.

Leaf. Light green and "transparent". Medium sized with fairly long petioles.

Plant. Upright growth and graceful form. Apparently a sport of the Mentor group.

Originated and Described: Jane B. Coleman, Georgia.

ORCHID BEAUTY (*Illustrated*)
Flower. Pale lavender-pink, fainter on margins. Small petals furled back, particularly upper two, and held slightly above leaves. Younger flowers exactly the same color as the older ones. Prolific. R.V.4
Leaf. Cordate, almost round and almost flat. Shiny, bright green above. Slightly pink below. Pinkish petioles, upright to a forty-five-degree angle.
Plant. Among the finest in or out of bloom.
Originated: R. A. Brown, Georgia.

ORCHID BEAUTY, DWARF (See Dwarf Orchid Beauty)

ORCHID GIRL
Flower. Light red-violet. Color and form same as Plum with cupped, slightly frilled petals, the upper two darker. R.V.3
Leaf. Same shape as Blue Girl but with less obvious variegation.
Plant. Spreading type.

ORCHID LADY
Flower. Orchid Beauty type. Small, furled back and pale lavender-pink. Held well above leaves. Prolific. R.V.6
Leaf. Cordate, small, dark green.
Plant. Closely resembles Orchid Beauty but leaves appear to be darker with flower stems longer. Flat rosette type.

Orchid
Beauty

PINK AMETHYST

Flower. Light violet-red, about six to a stem. Held well above foliage on rosy stems. Medium-sized.

Leaf. Dentate and sharply tapered from a cordate base. Medum-sized and medium to dark green, purplish beneath. Petiole three to four inches long and usually at a thirty- to forty-five-degree angle.

Plant. Upright grower. Frequently called a Westcoast "Amethyst" variety with lighter flowers. (Described by Ferne Kellar)

PLUM (*Illustrated*) (See page 178)

Flower. Orchid or light red-violet with bicolor tendency, two upper petals (R.V.2) always darker than three lower (R.V.3 to 5). Medium-sized and slightly cupped. Held well above leaves. Petals with uneven edges. Stem rosy. Older flowers less likely to fade than Trilby. Young flowers not much darker than mature ones but occasionally appear intense violet-red. R.V.2 and R.V.4

Leaf. Rhombic-ovate (widest at middle) with regular shallow crenation. All more or less convex, even young ones. Surface a bit lumpy. Medium green with slight sheen, pale below. Pinkish petioles, horizontal or drooping.

Plant. A handsome plant with large, convex leaves drooping over the edge of the pot.

Plum

Plum Satin (syn. Dark Plum)

Flower. Medium red-violet, upper two petals slightly darker. Medium-sized. R.V.3

Leaf. Ovate, obtuse base with small light spot at base. Shallow regular crenation. Shiny, medium green above and pale below. Petiole light.

Plant. Crisp and flat-looking.

Red Bicolor (syn. Bicolor, *Illustrated*)

Flower. Red-violet range with two upper petals consistently intense red-violet, darkest at tips. Lower three pale orchid-pink, sometimes with a slight deepening around edges. Young flowers darker all over than mature ones. Medium-sized. R.V.1 and R.V.4

Leaf. Large, flat, and dull. Veins rosy on underside.

Plant. Large, upright grower.

Originated: Charles Merkel and Sons, Ohio.

Redhead

Flower. Medium red-violet, shaped like Plum but with even more red in them than in young blooms of Plum. R.V.3

Leaf. Ovate and rather flat. Dull green, pale below.

Plant. Good appearance, typical of plants in the Plum-Trilby group.

Originated: Charles Merkel and Sons, Ohio.

Red Bicolor

REDLAND
Flower. Light red-violet. Medium-sized on long stems held well above foliage. R.V.3
Leaf. Resembles Amethyst. Ovate-cordate, acute, crenate. Medium-sized. Light to medium green. Rose-tinted below with darker veins.
Plant. Compact rosette. Sport of Amethyst.
Originated: J. A. Peterson and Sons.

TRILBY (*Illustrated*)
Flower. Lavender-pink or orchid. Similar to Plum with color varying considerably, depending on season and age of blooms. Young flowers are red-violet with upper petals darker. Mature flowers fade to lavender-pink. All may show bicolor tendency with very dark petal tips. Medium-sized. Stems rosy. R.V.3-4.
Plant. Flat growth with close, dull leaves. Sport of Blue Boy.
Originated: Glen St.Mary Nursery, Florida.

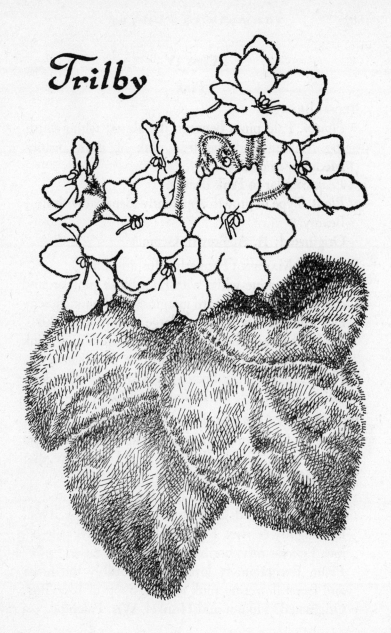

Trilby

Class IV

Pink

BLUSH BEAUTY

Flower. Pale pink, between the almost white Blushing Maiden and the true pink of Pink Beauty. Medium-sized. R.5

Leaf. Similar to Pink Beauty.

Plant. Type of growth apparently identical with Pink Beauty.

Originated: R. A. Brown, Georgia.

BLUSHING MAIDEN (Formerly Blushing Lady)

Flower. Opaque white with faint blush pink around center and fading toward margins. Pistil pink. Resembles Pink Beauty. Cupped, large, and prolific. R.6

Leaf. Thin and light green leaves resembling Pink Beauty. Irregularly bent. Whitish or pale below.

Plant. Same as Pink Beauty, very lovely.

Originated: Ulery Greenhouses, Ohio.

PINK BEAUTY (*Illustrated*)

Flower. True pink and large. Held high among and above leaves. Petals slightly cupped with irregular edges. Prolific. R.4

Leaf. Ovate or rhombic (broadest at middle and tapered at both ends). Shallow regular scallops. Thin, flat, slightly convex. Light dull green above, pale below. Petioles rosy, horizontal, or slightly raised.

Plant. Exceptionally lovely and probably the finest and freest flowering pink to date. Sport of Blue Boy.

Originated: Holton and Hunkel, Wis. Patented.

Pink
Beauty

Pink Girl

Flower. Somewhat deeper pink than Pink Beauty. The two upper petals are larger, having a slight ruffled edge. Medium-sized, cupped flowers. R.4

Leaf. Blue Girl type with some misshapen and twisted suggesting Curly Special. Irregular variegation and blotching. Shiny, medium green leaves with short hairs. Appears almost glabrous or devoid of hairs.

Plant. Similar to Pink Beauty.

Originated: R. G. Baxter, Ohio. Patent pending.

Pink Star (syn. Star Pink)

Flower. Small star-shaped and clear pink. Petioles erect holding blossoms well above leaves.

Leaf. Light green, ovate, and hairy. Inclined to cup downwards.

Plant. Collector's item and very rare. Similar to Pink Beauty.

Originated: R. A. Brown, Georgia.

Class V

White

White Lady (*Illustrated*)

Flower. Translucent white, glistening in some lights. Medium-sized, twisting, occasionally upside down. Usually crowded among leaves. Prolific.

Leaf. Ovate, shallow crenation. Margins curled down, twisted. Light dull green above, almost white below. Petioles pale, at every angle to vertical.

Plant. A bunchy grower, delightful and worth-while.

Originated: Silver Terrace Nursery, California. Patented by Fred C. Gloeckner, New York.

White Lady

Classification by Groups

Group A. Doubles

Double Blue Boy   Double Russian   Duchess

Group B. Bicolors

Red Bicolor (syn. Bicolor)

Group C. Miniatures

Lilac Lady   Dwarf Orchid Beauty (?)

Group D. Variegateds

Blue Girl   Pink Girl   Orchid Girl
Blue Girl Supreme

Group E. Novelties

Blue Chard   Curly Special   Ruffles

Compilation of Varieties

Here are the names of every African violet ever christened—at least to my knowledge. Undoubtedly there is duplication here and a measure of phantasy too, but it seemed interesting at one point in time to list the many names that have come my way. The varieties which have certain identity comprise a smaller list. These are described in the pages preceding and are marked below according to their classification.

Admiral
Afterglow
Agate
Albino
Alice Blue Gown
Alma's Blue
Amarantha
Amazon Blue
Amazon Pink
Amethyst (syn. Dark Amethyst) II
Amethyst, Improved or Spooned II
Amethyst Pink (See Pink Amethyst)
Azure Glory
Apple Blossom
Begonia Bell
Bicolor (See Red Bicolor)
Blue Barbara
Blue Beauty
Bluebelle
Blue Bird I

Blue Bobby (syn. Blue No. 2)
Blue Bonnet
Blue Boy I
Blue Boy Improved
Blue Boy Profuse
Blue Boy Supreme I
Blue Chard I E
Blue Darling
Blue Eyes II
Blue Flute I
Blue Girl I D
Blue Girl Supreme I D
Blue Jane
Blue Monday
Blue Scoop (syn. Chicago Scoop) I
Blue S-32 (Probably "32")
Blue Supreme
Blue Treasure (Formerly Blue No. 3)
Blue Velvet
Blush Beauty IV
Blue and White

Blushing Lady (*See* Blushing Maiden)

Blushing Maiden (Formerly Blushing Lady) IV

Bronze

Chicago Scoop (*See* Blue Scoop)

Commander I

Commando III

Commodore III

Crinkles I

Curly Special I E

Curly Twist

Dark Amethyst (*See* Amethyst)

Dark Plum (*See* Plum Satin)

Dickson Purple

Double Blue Boy I A

Double Orchid Beauty

Double Pink Beauty

Double Purple

Double Sport Blue Boy Supreme

Double Russian I A

Dubonnet

Duchess (Probably Double Blue Boy) I A

DuPont Amethyst III

DuPont Blue

DuPont Blue Boy Supreme

DuPont Lavender Pink (Formerly duPont Pink) III

DuPont Pink (*See* duPont Lavender Pink)

DuPont, Mrs.

DuPont Supreme, Mrs.

DuPont Red

DuPont, Will K.

Dwarf Orchid Beauty III C

Enchantress

Frieda III

Garnet

Good's Orchid

Gorgeous III

Guam

Hardee Blue

Heavenly Blue

Hyacinth Blue

Imperial

Improved Neptune (*See* Neptune Improved)

Improved Norseman

Ionantha II

Ionantha Grandiflora

Ionantha Improved

Jade

Janie's Blue

Jessie

Judy

Kewensis

Larene

Lavender

Lavender Lady

Lilac Lady III C

Lilac Lass

Lily Pad

Lithcum

Maiden's Blush (Probably Blushing Maiden)

Marine II

Mary

Mary Wac III

Mentor Boy I

Mentor Sport

Merkels Red

Mermaid

Mrs. Bowles
Myrtle II
My Second Prize III
Neptune I
Neptune, Dwarf
Neptune Spooned or Improved I
New Blue
New Double Purple
Norseman I
Norseman Lilac
Nosegay
Orchid Beauty III
Orchid Flute (Formerly du-Pont Orchid Flute) II
Orchid Girl III D
Orchid Lady
Orchid Queen (See Orchid Beauty)
Orchid Supreme
Ozark Skies
Pansy Purple I
Pansy Purple Supreme
Pink Amethyst (syn. Amethyst Pink) III
Pink Beauty IV
Pink Girl IV D
Pink Lady
Pink Perfection
Pink Purple (see Rose Purple)
Pink Star (syn. Star Pink) IV
Pink supreme
Plum III
Plum Pink
Plum Satin (syn. Dark Plum) III
Purple Beauty I

Purple Mist (may be synonymous with Mentor Boy) I
Purple Prince I
Red Bicolor (syn. Bicolor) III B
Red Bird
Red Girl (See Redhead Girl)
Redhead III
Redhead Girl (syn. Red Girl)
Redland III
Rose Purple (probably Pink Purple) I
Royal
Ruffles II E
S-22 Bicolor
Sailor Boy
Sailor Boy Improved
Sailor Girl
Sapphire I
Sky Blue (syn. Tinted Lady) II
Spooned Amethyst (See Amethyst Spooned)
Spooned Neptune (See Neptune Spooned)
Star Pink (See Pink Star)
Supreme I
Summer Skies II
Thirty-two "32" I
Tinted Lady (See Sky Blue)
Topaz I
Trilby III
Trilby Plum Pink
Turquoise I
Twilight
Variegated Leaf Sport
Velvet Beauty
Viking I

Waterlily II (syn. Starlight)   White Queen
White Beauty   White Sister
White Lady V   White Supreme
White King   Zig

Report of Classification Committee of the African Violet Society of America, Inc., meeting at Cincinnati, May 20, 1948:

Double Blue Boy, Double Russian, Duchess, and Silver Wings are the same variety and to be listed in alphabetical sequence.

Betty Joe, Mary Wac, Plum, Plum Pink, Plum Vivid, Orchid Queen, Rosy Blue, Trilby, and Vivid Plum are the same variety and to be known under the oldest name of Orchid Beauty. [The variety would not be the plant described as Orchid Beauty in this text but the Plum of page 164.—Author]

Commodore and Commander are the same variety and to be known as Commodore.

Glossary

Acute. A leaf terminating in a sharp point.

Anther. The small sac carried on a thread emerging from the center of each flower. The anther splits to release pollen grains containing the male elements of the plant.

Anthocyanin. A pigment which gives red, purple, or blue color to flower, leaf, or other parts of a plant.

Basic Slag. A slag low in silica and high in base-forming oxides.

Calyx. The outer series of floral leaves. This external part is usually green in contrast to the inner showy portion, or corolla, composed of colored petals.

Chromoplast. A pigment which gives yellow, orange, red, or brown color to flower, leaf, or other parts of a plant.

Cordate. A leaf form roughly heart-shaped and notched at the base.

Crenate. A leaf margin marked by rounded scallops.

Crock. A fragment of a broken, earthen flowerpot. If you fit a few overlapping pieces together in the bottom of a container to form a drainage area through which water but not soil will pass, you call it "crocking."

Cutting. A piece cut or broken from a parent plant for the purpose of obtaining additional plants of the identical type of the parent.

Dentate. A leaf with a toothed margin.

Entire. A smooth-edged leaf without grooves, scallops, or indentations of any kind.

Flat. A shallow box in which seeds or cuttings are started. The usual size is sixteen by twenty-two inches with a two-to-four-inch depth. Bottom boards are separated one-quarter inch to permit drainage.

Genus. (Plural, *genera*)   One subdivision of a plant family.

Germination. The first development of seeds into little plants. The rate of "bursting into life" depends not only on cultural factors but also on the innate disposition of the variety of the seeds.

Glucose. A sugar substance which occurs in nature.

Glucoside. A chemical group which when broken up into less complex substances yields the sugar glucose, or some other monosacharose, and certain other compounds.

Hydroponics. The science of growing plants in a solution of chemicals and without soil.

Midrib. The central vein of a leaf which appears as a ridgelike extension of the petiole or leaf stem.

Monosacharose. A simple sugar substance which occurs in nature.

Obovate. A leaf broader beyond the middle than at the base.

Obtuse. A leaf which is blunt rather than sharply pointed.

Ovate. Egg-shaped leaves attached to their stems at the broad end. (Cf. cordate leaves which are similar but notched at the base where the petiole joins.)

Petiole. The leaf stalk by which a leaf is attached to a main stem.

Pinching. The act of nipping out with thumb and finger the end growth of a branch, or removing tight little buds to make remaining development fuller, or to delay flowering.

Pistil. The ovule-bearing organ which receives pollen and, after fertilizing, develops seeds.

Plunge. The sinking of potted plants up to the pot rims in soil.

Pollen. The fertile, usually yellow dust, released from anthers.

Potbound. The condition of a plant actually filling with roots the container in which it is growing. If the pot is lifted from such a plant, a mass of roots is revealed covering the outside of the soil.

Sepal. A division of the calyx, that usually green cup which surrounds the colored petals.

Shifting. The moving of a plant to the next, larger-sized container with a little more soil but the least possible disturbance. This is in contrast to repotting which may involve replacement of worn-out soil with a fresh mixture, the improvement of drainage conditions, and even some cutting back of roots. Shifting is for healthy young plants on their way to maturity. Repotting is for established plants in need of reconditioning. In repotting a larger pot may be provided, the same one used again, or even a smaller one selected, if the previous pot was overlarge.

Sinus. A point at the base of a leaf scallop or crenation.

Species. This is something nature produces, a group of plants sharing certain distinctive characteristics which indicate a common parent or genus. In plant designation, the first word indicates the genus, the second the species to which it belongs, and the third the variety, as Saintpaulia ionantha, Blue Boy.

Stamen. The anther and the filament containing the male fertilizing cells.

Stigma. The sticky part of the pistil of a flower which receives and holds the pollen grains and on which they germinate.

Sub-irrigation. Watering from the saucer or below the surface of the soil.

Variety. The slight variation within a species which is noticeable but not important enough to constitute another species.

Index